Advances in Information Security

Network Security Policies and Procedures

Advances in Information Security

Sushil Jajodia

Consulting Editor
Center for Secure Information Systems
George Mason University
Fairfax, VA 22030-4444
email: jajodia@gmu.edu

The goals of the Springer International Series on ADVANCES IN INFORMATION SECURITY are, one, to establish the state of the art of, and set the course for future research in information security and, two, to serve as a central reference source for advanced and timely topics in information security research and development. The scope of this series includes all aspects of computer and network security and related areas such as fault tolerance and software assurance.

ADVANCES IN INFORMATION SECURITY aims to publish thorough and cohesive overviews of specific topics in information security, as well as works that are larger in scope or that contain more detailed background information than can be accommodated in shorter survey articles. The series also serves as a forum for topics that may not have reached a level of maturity to warrant a comprehensive textbook treatment.

Researchers, as well as developers, are encouraged to contact Professor Sushil Jajodia with ideas for books under this series.

Additional titles in the series:

Additional information about this series can be obtained from
http://www.springer.com

Network Security Policies and Procedures

by

Douglas W. Frye
SkilledAnalytics.com
USA

 Springer

Douglas W. Frye
SkilledAnalytics.com
Alexandria, VA, USA
dougfrye@yahoo.com

Network Security Policies and Procedures by Douglas W. Frye

ISBN-13: 978-1-4419-4047-6

e-ISBN-10: 0-387-47955-4
e-ISBN-13: 978-0-387-47955-2

Printed on acid-free paper.

9 8 7 6 5 4 3 2 1

springer.com

Table of Contents

List of Figures

Preface

Technology is progressing at an astounding pace, and many organizations are working so hard to implement the technologies they need to survive need to understand how their network security policies and procedures regimen fits into the picture.

As with all technology nowadays, the next significant change is already beginning to happen. As Service Oriented Architectures become the new reality and compliance regimes mature, the role of security as a portion of the enterprise as a whole will become more and more critical.

Ultimately, however, is the requirement for senior executives to understand how everything fits together. In the end, it is not enough to know you've deployed XYZ solution, but that the security regime as a whole in your organization is effective, how it aids in compliance, and how it impacts your business processes. By synthesizing communication, Enterprise Architecture and technology into a single volume, I have attempted to paint as complete a picture as possible about the security environment of the modern organization. I hope it contributes to the discussion on the subject.

Doug Frye
Alexandria, VA

Acknowledgments and Dedication

I would first like to thank Springer for granting me the opportunity to write this book for them. Ms. Susan Lagerstrom-Fife and her assistant, Ms. Susan Palleschi, have displayed saintly patience and have always been there when I needed them. My agency, StudioB, has been a constant source of support in my writing career, and I thank my (now former) agent Laura Lewin and Dr. Neil Salkind for their efforts in this and my other StudioB projects.

My family has also been a solid foundation for me. My dad David, my mom Jane and my identical twin brother Curt are always there for me.

Since Springer and I agreed that this project was a good idea, my life has become exponentially more complex. My job at Enterprise Integration, Inc. has grown as I have grown within the company. I thank Drs. Tom Gulledge and Ray Sommer for their mentoring over the years.

Finally, I am lucky to be completing this book now, as my wedding is only nine days away! I can't wait to begin my life with you, Debbie, and I dedicate this book to you. You'll be a wonderful mother, so the added level of complexity of children will be a treat.

Chapter 1 Information Technology and Its Role in the Modern Organization

Chapter Objectives

This chapter will discuss:
- The role information technology plays in an organization going about its daily business,
- The three basic employee types as referred to in the book: Managers, Technical Workers (IT specialists) and Non-Technical Workers,
- The role policies play in communicating an organization's priorities to its employees,
- Examples of incidents that have brought security and accountability to the fore, and
- The book's organization.

1.1 Information Technology's Role in an Organization's Processes

Over the past few decades information technology's (IT) ability to facilitate an organization's business processes has increased dramatically. From "electrifying" regular office tasks such as correspondence and allowing for storing the product virtually to Enterprise Resource Planning (ERP) and the newly emerging Service Oriented Architectures (SOAs), business is becoming more and more dependent on IT. It is critical for an organization to implement IT in a way that maximizes its benefit, but it is just as important that a regime of policies protecting the "corporate knowledge" be put in place to ensure that knowledge isn't stolen by outsiders.

In the past, computer and network security was the domain of the technical "folks in the lab". Executives and general employees did not know nor likely did they care what the network security people did to secure the company's systems as long as nothing was broken into and there was negligible downtime. Over the years, however, myriad factors have emerged to threaten a company's stability through compromising security. Stealing trade secrets and proprietary data are two examples of critical damage that can be inflicted upon a company when security is breached. Because many companies are interconnected with geographically distant sites as well as partner firms, and allow their employees to access internal systems from mobile devices such as laptops and Personal Digital Assistants (PDAs), there are ample targets for a potential intruder to select from when planning an attack. Unfortunately, simply guarding one's borders from outside intrusions is not enough today, as a substantial proportion of security violations are committed by someone within the victimized organization itself.

1.1.1 Cats and Dogs (Technical Workers and Management)

Technical workers and management tend to have one thing in common: they don't appreciate the constraints the other works within when going about their jobs. Management criticizes the system administrators for not understanding how the best technical solution isn't appropriate for meeting the company's goals, while the system administrators criticize management for not understanding that what they're asking for is impossible, overly expensive or foolhardy. While some counter-examples do exist in the IT world, quite often those in charge of running a business or governmental organization are professional managers rather than professional technologists with managerial training. Most of the time, those charged with constructing and implementing the technical architecture do not understand the business environment in which their organization is operating. After all, their job is to simply build what they're told to build, so what difference does it make if they understand the business context or not?

The above situation manifests itself in which courses in the required "core curriculum" we hated to take. If one couldn't stand the required public speaking or history classes because they got in the way of time spent in front of a computer, chances are there is no real understanding of the overarching mission of the organization. If calculus nearly ended a college career, in contrast, that person is not as likely to have a solid grounding in the technical aspects of how IT enables the organization's functions. Readers of this book will have a better understanding of how both areas come together to form a technical and policy regime to best serve the interests of the organization through the best possible mix of maximizing technical solutions while conforming to government and organizational requirements. Ultimately, this book's aim is to educate readers from both the technical and management communities. To an IT professional reading this book, the technical information will be very basic. To a manager, the communication aspects will be topics with which they are very familiar. When the reader considers the parts of the book addressing their area or non-expertise, however, it is hoped they will gain insight into how the entire picture fits together.

1.1.2 Non-Technical Workers Are a Key Consideration

The actions of non-technical workers who will likely never read this book are equally critical in safeguarding a company's security. These workers are often the target of con artists employing what has become known as "social engineering" (discussed in detail in Chapter 12) to gain access to company systems or information. A strong training and ongoing communication process to maintain a highly vigilant workforce through awareness is indispensable. Discussed in Chapter 16 will be several aspects of what motivates an employee as they go about their daily work. For this book's intended audience, though, it is important to remember that these workers are often the "front line" of the battle to keep a company's data within its own walls, and those to whom these policies must be communicated and against whom sanctions will be levied for violating them. It is not enough, nor is it fair; to answer a question asking why is it important to follow a particular policy with an answer that basically says "because we say so" or "because you'll be fired if you don't." To avoid these questions in the first place, a training regimen should educate all workers on a policy's relevance, but should they forget or not understand it is then incumbent upon the person asked the question to have the answer at hand or to be able to direct the worker to the policy's justification while still on the phone with them or by directing them to an online version of the policy statement while with them at their workstation.

The consequences of a company failing to maintain accurate, secure data is not simply a matter of competitive advantage. Tough new federal laws now impose severe penalties for false financial data and inadequately protected personal health information, for example. In all, a company is compelled to pursue aggressively a robust network security regime. This book's purpose is to leave the reader with a strong, multi-disciplinary understanding of how to best go about accomplishing this goal.

1.2 The Role Policies Play in an Organization

Policies and procedures are a critical part of an organization's being. Imagine an organization without a well-defined sexual harassment policy.

One wouldn't think it's possible a company would leave itself vulnerable to the legal jeopardy of facing a situation involving sexual harassment without having a policy forbidding it in place. The same should be true for protecting its data. As will be discussed in Chapter 8, investor lawsuits and two recent federal statutes, the Sarbanes-Oxley (SOX) and Health Information Privacy and Accountability Act (HIPAA) are serious requirements for organizations to take into consideration when determining how to go about organizing its policy regime.

Policies, it should be noted, affect different levels of an organization. In fact, senior leadership should be charged with setting the basic network security goals and allow its management team to "fill in the blanks" of how to actually implement the means through which the goals will be achieved. An effective way to accomplish this objective comes through combining two types of modeling: business process and balanced scorecard.

1.3 Incidents That Have Made Security and Accountability Major Issues

Recent developments in the U.S. have made the environment for an organization's senior leaders quite restrictive insofar as that they are being held much more accountable for alleged fraud and unauthorized release of protected personal data, for two examples. On the fraud side of the equation, the recent convictions of Bernie Ebbers, Jeffrey Skilling and Ken Lay in multi-billion dollar cases should have given executives pause, as they are now compelled to certify that the financial statements are accurate. As seen in Chapter 12, however, the data an organization possesses can be quite valuable to unscrupulous people for committing, for example, identity theft.

Marriott, for example, discovered that around 206,000 customers had their "credit card details, Social Security numbers, and, in a few cases, (their) bank details" compromised. (Marson, 2006) This incident occurred when a backup tape containing the data was lost from an office in Florida. Marriott apologized and offered to enroll all potentially impacted customers in a credit-monitoring service at no charge to help them check for unauthorized activity using their accounts. (ibid)

ChoicePoint, a data broker which sold data it had collected to "private investigators, debt collectors or businesses such as check-cashing outfits, unless they were associated with an accredited bank" because the data of approximately 145,000 people had been leaked to scam artists, and had resulted in no fewer than 750 cases of identity theft. (Evers, 2005(1))

Wired.com reported on several incidents (2005):

> "CitiFinancial, the consumer finance division of Citigroup...has begun notifying 3.9 million U.S. customers that computer tapes containing information about their accounts—including Social Security numbers and payment histories—have been lost.

> "Citigroup...said the tapes were lost by the courier UPS in transit to a credit bureau.

> "The bank said the tapes contained information about both active and closed accounts at CitiFinancial's branch network."

Additionally:

> "Last month, media and entertainment company Time Warner said computer backup tapes containing data on 600,000 individuals were lost by an outside data storage firm. The data covered current and former employees going back to 1986, as well as some of their dependents and beneficiaries, the company said." (ibid)

> "Also in May, more than 100,000 customers of Wachovia and Bank of America...were notified that their financial records may have been stolen by bank employees and sold to collection agencies. And in April, Ameritrade Holding, a leading online discount broker, said it had informed some 200,000 current and former customers that a backup computer tape with personal information had been lost." (ibid)

The most notable incident as of this writing, however, was an incident at CardSystems Solutions resulting in over 40 million credit card accounts being exposed.

> "The data security breach, possibly the largest to date, happened because intruders were able to exploit software security vulnerabilities to install a rogue program on the network

of CardSystems Solutions, MasterCard International spokeswoman Jessica Antle said. The program captured credit card data, she said.

"The malicious code was discovered after a probe into the security of CardSystems' network. That investigation, by security experts from Cybertrust, was triggered by a MasterCard inquiry into atypical reports of fraud by several banks. The trail led to CardSystems, Antle said.

"The probe also found that the Atlanta-based payment processor did not meet MasterCard's security regulations. CardSystems held onto records that it should have discarded, and it stored transaction data in unencrypted form, Antle said." (Evers, 2005 (2))

Data theft is not the only concern for organizations, however. Many will remember how e-mails from Bill Gates at Microsoft were used against him in the anti-trust case brought against the company by the U.S. federal government. Reuters (2005) reported on two incidents in which failure to retain e-mails for the required time period can lead to harsh penalties:

"Banks and broker-dealers are obliged to retain e-mail and instant messaging documents for three years under U.S. Securities and Exchange Commission rules. But similar requirements will apply to all public companies from July 2006 under the Sarbanes-Oxley corporate reform measures...

"(the recent) $1.45 billion verdict against Morgan Stanley in West Palm Beach, Fla., was the product of just such a negative ruling on e-mail retention...

"Circuit Court Judge Elizabeth Maass, frustrated at Morgan Stanley's repeated failure to provide (billionaire Ronald) Perelman's attorney's emails, handed down a pretrial ruling that effectively found the bank had conspired to defraud Perelman when he sold (his company) Coleman to appliance maker Sunbeam in 1998."

In the other case:

"U.S. District Judge Shira Scheindlin found that Swiss bank UBS had willfully destroyed potential e-mail evidence in a sex discrimination case brought by equity saleswoman Laura Zubulake. The judge ordered UBS to pay Zubulake's costs, and a jury later awarded her $29.2 million.

"Experts said e-mail retention could be a double-edged sword if not accompanied by corresponding training for employees on the legal implications of e-mails they send. (ibid)

The detail that should jump out at the reader is that no two circumstances were the same, and in several of the examples the loss was not the direct result of a mistake made by the company whose data was lost. In the case of judgments being made against companies for failing to produce e-mails as a part of discovery in legal proceedings, e-mail and instant messaging (IM) document retention can be a critical factor in determining damages in the millions of dollars due to a plaintiff. There are many, many ways in which an organization can be compromised legally in today's environment. It is the aim of this book to introduce the major elements that comprise an organization's connectivity, laws governing data produced and stored by IT systems, and a means of evaluating whether the organization is governing itself adequately.

1.4 The Book's Organization

The book follows a traditional organizational path by first introducing the basic elements involved in an organization's existence in today's IT environment. Chapter 2 describes at a high level the types of people involved in an organization's activities and the information they need to do their jobs. Chapter 3 introduces the reader to the physical components in an organization's connectivity. Chapters 4 and 5 detail the basics of what constitutes legitimate and illegitimate network access and the various means involved to gain the access. Chapter 6 is a discussion of encryption, how it works and the concerns government has relative to national security.

The two following chapters delve into organizational and governmental policy. Chapter 7 covers the Balanced Scorecard, an organizational governance methodology used to create a "control environment" capable of establishing the roles and responsibilities of all actors in an organization's business processes. Chapter 8 is a discussion of two recently-implemented U.S. laws. Sarbanes-Oxley (SOX) is a financially oriented statute that has come about as a direct result of the large-scale corporate fraud cases in the U.S., such as Enron and MCI-WorldComm. The Health Information Privacy and Accountability Act (HIPAA) addresses the protection of personal medical data.

Chapters 9 and 10 deal with two of what many consider the mundane details of network security: physical security and disaster recovery. While neither is a scintillating topic to deal with, they are no less important than implementing the world's best firewall. If someone is able to gain access to an organization's facility and bypass the firewall, it's worthless. In the same vein, if a disaster such as a flood or fire causes a facility to shut down and destroys equipment and data, an organization must have a plan in place to ensure operations may continue.

Chapters 11 and 12 shift the emphasis to the individual employee. Chapter 11 discusses the communication that should occur between the organization and an incoming employee through such instruments as a Non-Disclosure Agreement (NDA) and a Non-Compete Agreement, which protect the organization from an employee transferring proprietary data to anyone not authorized by the organization to receive it as well as prohibiting the employee from competing against the organization for a set period of time after the employee's tenure with the organization has ended. Chapter 12 moves into the realm of social engineering, with details on how it works and how it can be resisted.

Chapters 13 through 15 emphasize more technical aspects of network security. Chapter 13 covers e-mail, instant messaging and a social engineering technique unique to these media, "phishing." Chapters 14 and 15 introduce the reader to policies and procedures to be used in network administration and network monitoring.

Chapters 16 and 17 cover communication within the organization as it applies to how the organization establishes the priority it places on security through its senior leaders' messages to employees. Focus is also placed on an economic theory which establishes how much effort an employee is willing to place on a given task or goal. Chapter 17 deals specifically with training within an organization.

Chapter 18 provides synthesis for the preceding chapters. As the discussion of the first seventeen chapters establish how an organization controls its activities to establish a secure network and ensure its information is adequately protected, the context of a "control environment" is used as the intellectual underpinning for the chapter. Finally, Chapter 19 provides draft policies which an organization may use as a reference in formulating its own.

It is worth noting that the term "organization" is used rather than "business" or "government agency" in most cases, as the discussion is directed to both types of organization.

Chapter 2 The Extent of an Organization's Connectivity

Chapter Objectives

This chapter will discuss:
- The evolution from isolated functions to business processes,
- Who requires access to an organization's networks, and
- From where they require the ability to access the networks.

2.1 Access in the Age of the Extended Enterprise

Over the past few decades, the ability to communicate with others electronically has advanced dramatically, leading to first the creation of the Internet and later the World Wide Web. The impact of this phenomenon on organizations concerning the pace of operations and the need for efficiency in their business processes is significant and will only become more so for the foreseeable future.

Originally a project of the U.S. Department of Defense (DoD) Advanced Research Projects Agency (ARPA), its task was to give various DoD activities the ability to share information through networked computers, hence eliminating the need to wait for surface mail to be delivered. As the cost of both computers (also originally developed by the U.S. Government) and connectivity decreased, private industry's ability to implement information technology grew.

Since its invention in the 1950s, the Internet has facilitated communication among an ever-increasing community of users—as costs have decreased and capabilities have risen, the applications developed for the medium have multiplied. One application is integrating the functions of an enterprise into an increasingly seamless data management system. Companies such as SAP and Oracle have developed applications to provide this data management system. As is typical, the private sector led the way in implementing information technology, but the U.S. Government is now experienced in procuring enterprise resource planning (ERP) systems.

Before IT evolved to the point at which geographically distant parties became able to communicate with each other in beyond talking to each other or faxing each other, the only way to gather information was from the individuals responsible for their particular functionality. These "stove-pipes", established based on how labor was divided at the time, were only concerned with their specific requirements and had little or no regard as to how their processes related to those of other parts of the organization, as shown in Figure 2.1. With ERP systems, the power of IT to enable an organization's business has literally exploded.

ERP systems give organizations the ability to streamline their supply chain and their front- and back-office business processes into a more "flat" or "seamless" regime leveraging IT's ability to distribute information to authorized (or unauthorized if one's not careful) parties to allow formerly functional smokestack sections of the organization instantaneously. For example, rather than a customer service employee being required to tele-phone or e-mail a colleague and wait for a response to a query, ERP solutions employ integrated applications with all information relevant to a cus-tomer user "case" available as shown in Figure 2.2. This real-time ability to access the most up-to-date information available as well as to generate reports based on that information is, according to Ptak (1999), critical to allowing decision makers to make good business decisions.

A major implication of a process-centric approach to information tech-nology implementation is that an organization will be forced to change its emphasis on how it rewards its employees from doing one's job in isola-tion to helping to enable the business process or processes in which they reside. In the public sector especially, it is extremely difficult to realize organizational change. Instead, the organization goes through great pains to maintain the status quo. Many in government remember the days when new systems were custom-built and implemented functionality as specifi-cally defined by the procuring organization's requirements. ERP systems, on the other hand, establish its options on already-coded best business practices and forces the organization to choose among available options, with "downstream" choices constrained by those made "upstream."

Business Processes

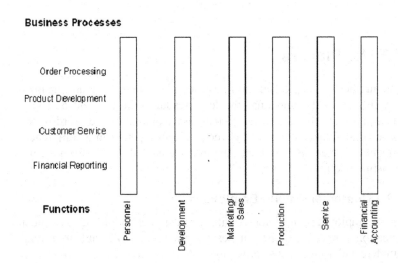

Figure 2.1 Non-ERP Enabled Processes (Adapted from Perez, et al, 1998)

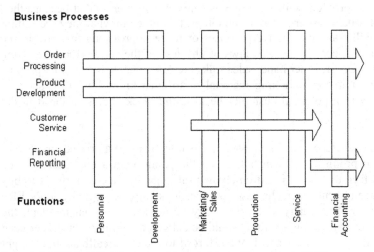

Figure 2.2 ERP Enabled Processes (Adapted from Perez, et al, 1998)

The next section discusses many of the "moving parts" of an organization required to access its IT systems.

2.2 The Players

The number of people and the roles they play in ensuring an organization fulfills all of its functional and legal responsibilities might be somewhat surprising to the reader, not in that they would not have heard of any of these actors but that they had never put them together in a comprehensive mental framework. In fact, this discussion is likely far from a complete listing itself.

2.2.1 Customer-Facing Employees

Those employees who interact with the customer should have as much information as possible at their disposal to allow them to be able to provide a complete and accurate answer to any customer inquiry.

Sales is one of the groups with which the rest of the organization has a love-hate relationship. Because sales folks are how much of a company's business is generated, everyone else relies on them to stay employed. A common problem with sales representatives, however, is that because they aren't usually experts in the technologies involved in what they are selling they will sometimes make promises or leave impressions that are, in the case of IT, contrary to the "laws of physics" of the system they are trying to sell. On the other hand, sales folks are often unable to generate proposals and tailored marketing material or to even know how to describe a product to a potential customer because they lack access to the data describing it.

Another issue sales associates face is how many of a product are "available to promise." When talking on the phone with a customer or even when face-to-face, it is extremely helpful in gaining a commitment to buy at that moment when the associate can look into the organization's ERP and know how many of an item may be purchased at that moment, the price per item and when they would be delivered. Should a customer need to hold for too long or if they are forced to receive a callback they might inquire with a competitor and place their order with them before the original company would be able to get back to them with an answer.

Marketing professionals have the responsibility to generate the material sales people and the organization's website use to promote their offerings to potential and existing customers. In order to do so and to keep the materials as up-to-date as possible, marketers have a need to know not only the most current information on each product available, but also what will be released in the foreseeable future. Marketing professionals, along with sales and the technical people who produce the products to be sold, staff the booths at trade shows and conferences, at which valuable contacts and sales leads are often generated. Marketers are often not as knowledgeable about the technical details of a product and as such will rely on an ability to provide a potential customer with a brochure or data sheet about the organization's offering, which would be generated most efficiently by accessing the product data directly from the system versus a "data call" from the product team.

Customer service representatives also have significant interaction with customers but will likely only know the history of the transaction in question by what they are able to access on their computer. In the case of a sales associate not being available to a customer, they will be able to call customer service to place their order or to inquire as to the price and availability of what they would like to purchase. In addition, customer service representatives will often be forced to deal with customer complaints, especially about overdue orders or those with quantity, quality and billing issues. For issues requiring the customer to return product, the process to receive return items, known as "reverse logistics", must be enabled. In this instance, the customer service representative must provide the customer with the ship-to address and often a code to include on the box or return invoice to give the receiving department the information it needs to enter the return in the system to enable credit minus any restocking fee to be applied to the customer's account.

Technical Support is both a customer-facing and internal job which, as the name suggests, helps callers (or e-mailers or chatters) resolve problems relating to the functionality of products they have bought from the company. In order for the tech support person to be able to assist the callers, they must know how to diagnose the problem in order to be able to turn to the correct "script" to guide the user through the repair process if they are not already familiar with it. In order to do this, diagnostic procedures followed by the technical data to fix the problem must be available within a few seconds to the representative, as quite often the customer must resolve the issue quickly in order to complete their task as soon as possible.

Technical support is a major candidate for what is known as "offshoring," or outsourcing to an overseas contractor in a country such as India, which has a large amount of highly trained technical experts who are far less expensive than domestic employees or contractors. Whether offshoring makes economic sense is beyond the scope of this book but is an issue to be considered when deciding whether to keep technical support in-house or to contract it out domestically or internationally.

2.2.2 Internal Functional Employees

Another type of worker under management is the "functional," who has a large hand in making sure the day-to-day workings of the organization go smoothly. In this section, those who actually make or design the product and those who enable the production are discussed.

Manufacturing and Production workers are what most people see in their minds when they are asked to picture a company employee, at least traditionally. These are the men and women who, for example, work the assembly line in an automobile plant. In the IT or "information worker" industries, they are the people who write the code or compose the documents that comprise the organization's products. Factory workers are the epitome of what was once the predominant economic model for an organization: tasks separated out to an extent that sometimes the individual worker did not know how what they did on a daily basis fit into the overall picture of the organization's mission. Because production workers mostly worked on a quota system, and were rewarded or punished based on whether or not they met the company's expectations, they had no reason to care how what they did contributed to the organization.

Now, while they still don't need to as much information as many other workers, they do need access to the IT systems to know what they are to make and how many of each. In many fields, such as the computer industry, the mix of product to be made each day can vary widely, and the factory worker must know what they will need to make that day or even that hour. The most efficient way for them to find out that information is by receiving it from the production planning system.

In today's age of the information worker, the business or production process they are within is critical knowledge. Despite their increased reliance on an IT system's output, factory workers typically have only one job to do at a time and that job has been integrated into the overall business process by someone else; it's not the line employee's job to think about it. For the information worker, however, it is imperative that they realize how what they do impacts the rest of the process. In an ERP implementation, for example, a decision on how to meet a specific requirement will influence or even dictate how another requirement is met. If the decision is not coordinated beforehand in a complex organization, such as the U.S. DoD, it may inadvertently cause the system to be non-compliant with a regulation or policy. Because of this, close communication and decision-making among senior leaders throughout the organization is needed from the start of the project.

Operations and Logistics are two other "hands-on" fields of work. In operations, employees ensure the infrastructure is in place for workers to be able to do their jobs, be it as simple as a new employee has a desk ready for them when they arrive or as complex as that the extremely expensive machine used to make the organization's product is running perfectly. Several bits of information are needed in operations. First, they either need access to or automatically generated reports from the human resources system to see if new employees are coming to the facility or if some are leaving in order to know if they need to order materiel to accommodate the incoming employee or if they may transfer something from the outgoing employee to the new arrival.

For the expensive machinery, operations must, for example, know when to take it offline for maintenance. To determine the maintenance schedule, operations must know from the production schedule when the best time to do so would be. If there is no "best time," the production planning system must be notified of when the system will be taken offline in order to allow the systems customers, customer service and sales access to be updated with accurate availability status and dates. If all this is accomplished automatically, it is seamless. If not, it is a potentially long process of manually accessing and updating several different systems, which leads to input errors and incomplete updates, meaning that the data in one system is different than the data in another system, which is disastrous. Instead, it is always preferable to rely on an "authoritative source" for each piece of data throughout the enterprise to ensure consistency (and assuming the single source is correct, of course).

Logistics professionals deal in the transport of materiel from one location to another, be it internally within the organization (such as from one location to another), from the organization to a customer, or in reverse logistics, in which the organization receives something it shipped out back from a customer. Because the shipping and receiving department is highly labor-intensive, and having too few or too many workers on hand to process the incoming and outgoing materiel is expensive, the scheduling system must know from the production planning system how much materiel is to be produced and shipped out on a given day or even during a given shift. In addition, incoming shipments must be received, including customer returns as discussed earlier. Some organizations, such as Wal-Mart, are moving to implementing Radio Frequency Identification (RFID) chips in their warehouses and stores (currently down to the pallet level), which will, when adequately mature, reduce reliance on humans to account for what has gone out and what has come in. In another example, one may remember the recent U.S. television commercial in which a Wal-Mart truck had its destination changed "mid-flight" to restock a store that had an urgent need for an item in the truck. When this happens, the logistics system must trigger the sending of the goods to its original destination on a future shipment.

2.2.3 Internal Support Employees

It is perhaps unfair to label this next group of employees as "support," because they do perform quite valuable functions for an organization, not the least of which is to help keep the company and its employees out of court and maybe jail, but the term applies in that these employees do not actually produce anything to be sold to or consumed by a customer.

Human Resources is the part of the organization in charge of administering its employment policies. Posting open positions and screening resumes is one part of the HR professional's duties, but it is also their purview to ensure all required documentation, such as non-disclosure agreements, non-compete agreements and all relevant policies (appropriate computer use, for example) have been signed and are on file. For many organizations, some of its work will require the employee to be approved for a billing category, have a security clearance or to have received training in a specialization, such as the handling of hazardous materials. In the U.S. military, by way of example, a combatant commander planning a mission or expecting a particular situation to arise will, among other things, check to make sure there are sufficient numbers of trained personnel at their disposal to undertake the mission or to deal with the anticipated situation should it come to bear.

Accounting is a thankless job, in that financial requirements are so well-defined and specialized that accounting's requirements and most everyday workers' view of what is adequate documentation is far from the same. As anyone who has had to correct an expense report or timesheet multiple times will attest, the level of negative feedback the accounting department receives is quite high. The biggest issue for them in dealing with employees, of course, is ensuring that all hours charged to the client and all expenses charged to the company or to the client are adequately documented to ensure the organization is able to pass an audit. For companies who are contractors to the U.S. government, the documentation requirements are quite strict and cumbersome. The information generated by the system, however, allows for managers and senior leadership to see if the expenditures on a contract or investment capital (also known as the "burn rate") is below, at or above the targeted rate. They also submit payroll and expense reimbursements, so we should all try to be as nice as possible to them.

Auditing is a department that strikes fear into even the most honest of employees, if nothing else for the sheer time-consuming nature of being involved in an audit. As will be discussed in Chapter 8, however, new laws stemming from the recent Enron scandal and the unintended release of private health and financial records require companies to establish that they are compliant with its mandates as enacted in federal regulations. This also impacts public sector implementations, as personal information as well as classified data, for example, must be protected.

2.2.4 Management

To many, "management" is simply an amorphous cloud of people to whom one must answer but whose function in the organization is unknown to the lower-level workers. In fact, managers at all levels have responsibilities that are key to the overall success of the organization. Three levels of managers and the type of information they require to do their job are summarized here. In many organizations there are many more levels, it should be noted.

Line managers, those who manage the workers, need to know the information generated by those under their direct supervision in order to report to the next level of managers above them. While this information can be many and varied, for purposes of simplifying it for this example, assume that it is simply a consolidation of all the output the workers in the manager's group produce. The managers are then responsible to their next level of supervision to demonstrate they are meeting their business goals as required to implement the organization's business processes. Line managers are typically responsible for approving timesheets and expenses as well as monitoring how their area of responsibility is performing regarding schedule and quality.

Middle management is the next level of accountability, and these managers are those who were traditionally in charge of the line managers within their functional area, which holds true in many organizations today. In other organizations, middle managers are part of the business process governance structure. Middle managers are required to coordinate with their peers from other parts of the organization to ensure decisions they make do not have negative impacts on other parts of the operation. To aid their analysis, middle managers have a need to see additional data from IT systems in order to allow them to confirm that their area of responsibility conforms with relevant laws and meets business objectives.

Senior management is charged with ensuring that large areas of the organization are working according to plan, such as the person in charge of security for the entire organization. In order to ensure all is well, senior managers will not often be required to see how individual functionalities are being performed but will rather need to have access to timely and accurate data "rolled up" into the measures they need to know their areas of responsibility are meeting objectives.

For all of the required access to information to happen, the business process, involved data, IT infrastructure and user roles must be modeled and configured precisely in order for the information to flow the way it must for someone to be able to have the data they need when they need it. This is the ideal state of affairs, obviously. Very few if any organizations have achieved this level of sophistication to this point; most will continue to rely on some sort of export or physical transfer of data to compile the reports workers need to be able to do or know how well they are doing their jobs and to be able to ensure their areas of responsibility will withstand an audit.

2.2.5 External Players

It is difficult at best for access within an organization to be controlled, but in this era of ubiquitous access and business process across an extended enterprise comprised of multiple organizations it is not always enough to have only one's own employees able to access its systems.

Suppliers, at the beginning of an organization's supply chain, need to know what they will be required to deliver and when. Companies such as Dell (as documented in Frye, 2004) have implemented systems which allow suppliers to know what they need and when they need it. Because the Dell's production planning is recalculated very often, suppliers are connected to the company's system to enable them to receive updates to the delivery requirements as quickly as they become available. Dell pushes a large amount of the inventory risk onto its suppliers, but it does its best to coordinate with the supplier to let them know the range of product they will need in order to allow them to plan their own purchases and production schedules.

Customers, at the other end of the supply chain, always have one question: "Where's my stuff and when is it going to get here?" In the U.S., customers are able to track many of their orders from Amazon.com from receipt of the shipping notification through delivery by, for example, UPS. UPS and FedEx have very good package tracking systems, to the point where one is able to trace the path of the package from where it leaves the Amazon distribution to the UPS distribution center from which it is delivered, when it goes out for delivery and when it was in fact delivered.

Just like with internal users but even more critical is the access external actors enjoy. Special care must be taken to ensure that those outside of the organization have no more information access than is absolutely necessary for them to do their jobs.

2.3 Locations from Which Access is Required

Today's extended enterprise in many cases reaches around the globe. In software development, for example, it is not uncommon for work to be done on project 24 hours each work day. Workers in California pass off their progress to programmers in India, who in turn send it to developers in Israel, for example. For an Intel computer chip, for example:

> "The process starts in Japan, where a single crystal is grown into a large ingot of silicon by Toshiba Ceramics. The silicon ingot is then sliced by suppliers, like Toshiba Ceramics or others, into thin wafers that are flown across the Pacific to one of Intel's semiconductor fabs in either Arizona or Oregon. At the fabs, hundreds of integrated circuits are etched and layered on each wafer, forming individual dies on the wafers. Finished wafers are packaged and then flown back across the Pacific to Intel's Assembly and Test Operations in Malaysia. The wafers are treated and cut into die, and the dies are finished into sealed ceramic 'packages.' The packages are then placed in sub-

strate trays that are put into Intel boxes and then packaged again in blank boxes (to conceal that they are Intel products) for shipment back across the Pacific to Intel warehouses in Arizona. Having traveled across the Pacific three times already, the chips are then shipped to Dell factories in Texas, Tennessee, Ireland, Brazil, Malaysia, and China, or one of its contract manufacturers in Taiwan, to be used as components in Dell computers. The journey ends when the product ships from Dell to the customer's home or office anywhere in the world, amounting to a fantastic and complex global voyage." (Sheffi, 2005)

The key point to remember based on the above discussion is that people in each location must know how much materiel is coming into the facility, when it will arrive, how many must be shipped to each location and when they must arrive. This process is highly coupled and, as Sheffi noted, very complex. There are also, for example, import/export, financial and security issues connected with many of the shipments.

2.3.1 Fixed Locations

As was seen in Sheffi's example, the creation and distribution of an Intel semiconductor is a very involved process. In a complex enterprise, there will be several facilities that will not change their physical location during the process. These plant sites, fabrication labs, distribution centers and others require current and accurate information to flow into them to enable them to plan. Multiple sites in the *same country* must communicate and are subject to domestic laws governing, for example, the transport of hazardous materials. Multiple sites in *multiple countries*, however, have this and other issues, such as import/export and data protection. At all times, however, in the newly-enabled extended enterprise, everyone with a need to know should be able to access the information from their desktop based on their role and the availability of data.

2.3.2 Mobile Locations

In the Intel example, there were several instances of the materiel traveling by boat across the Pacific. What if rough seas were to delay the shipment's arrival? With satellite communications, the facility expecting the shipment and all those who need to know can be updated quickly with a new estimated time of arrival. The advantage to being able to do so is that the receiving facility is now able to reschedule its work based on the up-to-date information and notify all involved in the enterprise of the revised delivery schedule.

2.3.3 Alternate Work Locations

Myriad ways to access an organization's systems with myriad devices are available to individuals at inexpensive costs by business standards. Discussed in future chapters, laptops, desktops, combination devices (cell phones and personal digital assistants for example) are all able to access an organization's IT systems.

Several places are available to a worker when they are not in the office:

- Home-Telecommuting is an option with many organizations now. This is convenient, especially in urban areas where commutes are routinely an hour or more each way, but it is also a challenge in that the worker's connectivity must be established in a way that the organization will be certain the employee is able to do their work without having access to more information than they are entitled to have, as this causes both competitive and compliance issues.
- Transport- Whether on a bus, train or in a car the commute is a good time to be productive for many workers, although functionality could be limited by the type of connection available.
- Public Access- Some eating establishments and bookstores in the U.S. offer complimentary wireless internet access, and many more serve as "hotspots" for services such as T-Mobile. Internet cafes, in which users rent access to a computer and the internet, are also popular.

2.4 Conclusion

The new world of IT as enabled by ubiquitous connectivity and ERP systems affords the opportunity for an organization to act much more efficiently than before by enabling business processes and their related data to be shared across the extended enterprise. For security professionals and senior leadership, the challenge of the new regime is to only allow those who have a legitimate right to access information to do so. To allow unauthorized access could have major competitive consequences and could also put those responsible in legal jeopardy, as will be discussed in Chapter 8's coverage of the Sarbanes-Oxley and HIPAA laws. The following chapters will discuss the infrastructure of an organization's IT networks, and in

Chapters 16 and 17, for example, the ways in which an employee may be informed of the importance of maintaining security and how they should be trained to properly protect proprietary information.

2.5 Discussion Questions

Think of the process one goes through in your organization to be reimbursed for expenses incurred.

- How many people are required to approve the submission before accounting is authorized to pay you?
- Do you need to fill out a paper form, an online form, or both?
- What form of documentation do you need to provide to prove you spent what you're claiming? Is there an amount below which you don't need to produce documentation or are there some instances in which the amount of your reimbursement is fixed?
- Do you receive payment by check or direct deposit into your bank account?
- If you know, how does the accounting department submit its reimbursement authorizations to the bank? Or does your organization use a payroll service?

Next, think of a key function you perform in your job (if you're a student, think of the process you go through to register for classes, but also add in the possibility that you may need to convince a professor to let you add the class you want even though the computer says its full.)

- Is there a standard procedure to accomplish what you need to do?
- Are there multiple paths to accomplish what you need to do?
- Can you create a flow chart of the process and all its possibilities?
- In your job do you know everyone to whom you might provide proprietary information? Do you have security procedures to follow to authenticate that the person requesting the information is entitled to have it?

How does your job fit into the overall mission of your organization? Why is it necessary? Which business processes do you support?

In how many ways are you able to access your organization's IT systems?

Do you have access to the IT systems of other organizations? Do any employees of other organizations have access to your IT systems?

Chapter 3 Network Physical Components

Chapter 3 Objective

- This chapter will discuss the various physical components of an organization's network.

3.1 Introduction

In a modern organization there will be a significant IT posture, relative to the size of the operation. While modern connectivity has improved an organization's ability to operate in an extended enterprise spanning all corners of the world, as discussed in Chapter 2, it has also put them at risk for theft, fraud, data loss and hacking, as the examples from Chapter 1 established.

To provide the background for the communication, policy and enterprise architecture discussions to follow in later chapters, the next few chapters will discuss the various physical and software-based elements of an organization's IT environment. Chapters 14 and 15 cover network administration and monitoring. As the emphasis of this book is on the policies facilitating a well-structured enterprise, the directly technical aspects of the issues are covered in sufficient depth to provide the reader with an overview of the subject matter.

3.2 Computers

3.2.1 Desktops and Laptops

Virtually everyone with an office job uses a computer for at least parts of their job, even if it is only as a typewriter substitute. The desktop computer (Figure 3.1) is the most common piece of hardware used to perform work and to access the Internet, while the laptop (Figure 3.2) is the choice of consultants, especially those who travel and must work on airplanes, in hotel rooms and on café tables, often with one or more colleagues sharing the space. Desktops are the more powerful of the two systems, but laptops now have capabilities sufficient to perform all routine work and at the high end have the ability to perform complex and resource-intensive functions such as economic analysis.

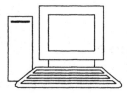

Figure 3.1 A Desktop Computer

Figure 3.2 A Laptop Computer

Laptops, however, are already starting to be replaced by what could still be considered early adopters of handheld computers, of which Personal Digital Assistants (PDAs) are the forerunners. PDAs that have multiple additional functions, such as email, phone and Internet access in addition to their contact management and calendar functionality, are becoming the norm in the office and (perhaps unfortunately) on trains and in restaurants.

3.2.2 Servers

Servers (Figure 3.3) are computers that house programs to be accessed by the workstations (desktops, laptops and handhelds) on the network.

Figure 3.3 A Server

Three common functionalities are:

- Web (Internet) server,
- Email server and
- Print server.

Important: Servers are sold able to support a significant number of processes which come enabled and with default passwords and user accounts. It is strongly suggested that all unneeded services be turned off, all unused user accounts be removed and all default passwords changed.

3.3 Connectors

There are several types of equipment used to allow IT devices to communicate (network) with each other. Several, including: hubs, switches, modems and routers are addressed below.

3.3.1 Hubs

Hubs connect multiple IT devices together on a network while eliminating the need to connect each computer to each other individually, as seen in Figure 3.4. The way the hub manages the traffic over the network is by coordinating the signals from each device so as to avoid or minimize "collisions" and fouled connections, but as traffic increases more and more collisions will occur. Hubs are extremely cheap and efficient for their intended purpose.

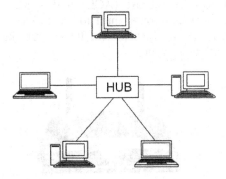

Figure 3.4 A Hub-Facilitated Network

3.3.2 Switches

Hubs and another device, the bridge, which divides traffic into different, non-conflicting areas, have largely been replaced in modern systems by the switch. Because of an enhanced ability to help network traffic from one device avoid colliding with that of another device through creating multiple "lanes" for the traffic. This also provides a layer of security, as someone tracking the network traffic would need to be "sniffing" multiple sources rather than a single one, as would be the case with a hub.

3.3.3 Modems

Modems are likely thought of as the devices which allow computers to communicate over phone lines. One of the earliest instances of those of us who grew up in the late 1970s and early 1980s is the movie *War Games*, starring a very young Matthew Broderick. In the movie, he placed his telephone headset on the modem (protected by "cups" to help maintain the connection) and dialed out on a fishing expedition ("wardialing") to find other computers. In recent years, the definition of a modem has been expanded to include a device receiving traffic from a Digital Subscriber Line (DSL) or cable internet service provider.

3.3.4 Routers

Routers (Figure 3.5) manage network traffic in a way that optimizes the network's efficiency. As network traffic is no longer sent as a continuous stream but as a series of "packets," the router is able to use optimization algorithms to decide the best path for each packet to take. The packets are re-assembled at the end of their trip back into their original form.

Routers may also serve a security function, as some are able to be equipped with Access Control Lists (ACLs) to deny passage to packets not on the ACL. If the rules a router must follow to know if a packet is allowed to continue are overly complex, there could be a "traffic jam" caused by the "bottleneck" router.

Figure 3.5 A Router

3.4 Firewalls

A *firewall*, as the term originally meant to the author, is a physical wall in an automobile that separates the engine from the passenger compartment, hopefully allowing the car's occupants some additional time to make their escape in case of an emergency. In the IT world, it serves a similar purpose by "inspecting and then approving or rejecting each connection attempt made between your internal network and external networks like the Internet. Strong firewalls protect your network at all software layers—from the Data link (such as Ethernet) layer up through the Network layer (such as TCP/IP) and up to the Application layer (such as HTTP)." (Strebe, 2004) In Figure 3.6, we see a firewall working as intended, repelling the hacker's penetration attempt, represented by the dashed line.

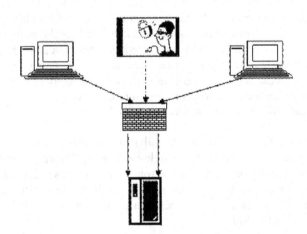

Figure 3.6 The Firewall (Ideally) Allows in the Legitimate Users But Keeps the Hacker Out

Strebe (ibid) notes that a modern firewall performs three basic functions:

- Packet filtering,
- Network Address Translation, and
- Proxy service.

A physical filter, such as the oil, air and fuel filters found in automobiles, screens out impurities before they foul the engine. The *packet filter* functionality performs an analogous function in that it prevents "impure" packets from reaching your computers. Filters typically operate by:

- "Dropping inbound connection attempts but allowing outbound connection attempts to pass.
- "Eliminating TCP packets bound for ports that shouldn't be available to the Internet...but allowing packets that are required to pass. Most filters can specify exactly which server a specific sort of traffic should go to—for instance, SMTP *(Simple Mail Transfer Protocol- author)* traffic on port 25 should only go to the address of a mail server.
- Restricting inbound access to internal IP ranges." (ibid)

Network Address Translation allows one to multiplex (reuse) a single IP address several times across a network. Because IP addresses are at a premium, smaller organizations are often not able to obtain large blocks of addresses and are thus forced to do what they can to make as many devices as possible able to access and be accessed by devices outside the organization. A drawback of NAT is that because a NAT server has only one "real" IP address serving several devices an outsider is unable to specify one of those devices as a receiver, and internal devices are unable to specify the client they want to connect to. (ibid)

The *proxy services* that a firewall provides stops someone trying to monitor your network from being able to do so by "making connections to the public Internet on behalf of internal private clients. Because application-layer proxies understand the specific protocol for which they proxy, they are able to detect and block malformed or maliciously modified streams." (Strebe, 2004)

3.5 Conclusion

The modern network has several components, which were introduced in this chapter. When it comes to security, routers and firewalls provide a good measure of protection against outside attackers. As mentioned during the routers discussion, making the security controls too tight could delay legitimate network traffic and reduce IT functionality to an unacceptably slow level. At all times the security level must be balanced against the need for the organization to be able to conduct its business in a timely manner.

3.7 Discussion Questions

What kind of IT network setup does your organization use?

Does your organization use a firewall? Does the software ever block traffic?

Are there ever conflicts between the business people and the IT security people over performance?

Chapter 4 Legitimate Network Access

Chapter 4 Objective

- This chapter will discuss the various ways in which a user may legitimately access an organization's network.

4.1 Introduction

There are several ways to gain access to a computer or network, but the concept of "authentication" is the same no matter what the means used. A user may authenticate themselves in one or a combination of three things:

- Something they *are,*
- Something they *know*, and/or
- Something they *have.*

4.2 The Three Somethings

4.2.1 Something You Are

In this means of authentication, a person establishes their identity in the same ways law enforcement does in identifying victims or suspects in their investigations. Known as *biometrics*, or measures of the body, they use the following devices:

- Microphone (voice recognition)- In many movies, voice identification has been used as a means for villains and heroes to gain access to what was thought to be an impenetrable room or facility. Now, technology has progressed enough that a "voiceprint" may be established and used as a means for accessing facilities and even computers.

- Optical scanners and electrostatic grids (fingerprint, handprint)- In Clarksburg, West Virginia, the U.S. Federal Bureau of Investigation has a large fingerprint "clearing house," at which they are able to analyze fingerprints from around the nation if not the world. While not as sophisticated or powerful, many computers now have a fingerprint scanner to be used as a means of unlocking a computer (in fact, these words are being written on a laptop with a fingerprint scanner).

- Digital video camera (facial features, retinal patterns)- It is said that a person's retina is as unique to themselves as their fingerprint. The retinal scans seen in movies such as *Demolition Man* and *Minority Report* are now an affordable reality. Facial recognition software is also used by such persons as private investigators for Las Vegas casinos to help the properties spot known cheats and other suspicious persons.

- DNA- In a U.S. commercial from a few years ago, a person attempting to access a computer first entered a password, then a fingerprint, then a drop of blood, and then a strand of hair. Unfortunately for the user, he was completely bald. While this method of verification is by far the least widespread of the authentication techniques discussed here, it is available. (Strebe, 2004)

Important: Unfortunately, biometric devices are still vulnerable to exploitation. For example, a high-resolution photograph of a fingerprint can still fool a fingerprint reader.

4.2.2 Something You Know

Password policies will be discussed later in the book, but here it is enough to know the following about passwords:

- They should not be based on a bit of personal information that is easily guessed (birthdates, etc.),
- They should be of sufficient length and should include "special characters", for example #^&, to help foil "brute force" attacks which try all possible combinations of letters/numbers/special

characters. The longer the passwords and the more complex, the exponentially tougher it is for a brute force attack to succeed.

- They should not be written on a sticky note and posted on your computer screen or taped to the bottom of your keyboard.
- They should not be the same for all of your accounts.

Many password policies in organizations are very strict, requiring long strings of characters and frequent changes. One technique to have them recorded somewhere is in an innocuous-looking file on your computer. This is dangerous, but it is the common reaction to needing to remember several different and difficult passwords.

4.2.3 Something You Have

The third general method for authenticating oneself is through something that provides you with a number or phrase to input that matches that stored by the computer. Known as "tokens," the concept was applied in the movie *A Beautiful Mind*, in which Russell Crowe's character, in his delusional state, believed that he had had a code generator implanted in his arm that he needed to input into a box to unlock it for passing on information about Soviet activities. This type of thing exists in real life in the form of a token issued by RSA, for example. The possessor of the token inputs the number on the token and is allowed access if the number input and that the computer believes is correct match.

4.4 Conclusion

This chapter, while brief, introduced the reader to the key concept of authentication. When used in combination, two or all three of the methods for a person to authenticate themselves with the machine provide a strong level of security against intrusion.

4.5 Discussion Questions

How many passwords do you have? Do you remember them all?

What are your organization's requirements for you to authenticate yourself? Do you use biometrics or a token? What do you think of those means of authentication?

Do you have alternate means of identifying yourself to your computer?

Chapter 5 Illegitimate Network Access

Chapter 5 Objective

This chapter will discuss:

- The "profiles" of those who illegitimately access systems,
- The various ways in which a user may illegitimately access an organization's network, and
- The various technical means an intruder may use to collect information or damage a target system.

5.1 Introduction

While there have been great strides in protecting ones networks, there remains a never-ending battle between those who wish to protect information those who wish to penetrate systems. Not all who penetrate systems do so maliciously, at least in their point of view, but from an organization's perspective anything that could cause damage is by its very nature malicious.

5.2 The Profiles

The human mind works best when it is able to segment people and things into clear groups. This is a fallacy, as no two people are alike and no two people are motivated identically. When considered in a broad context and used simply for discussion purposes, however, certain profiles of attackers hold true for someone in charge of defending an organization's IT systems.

5.2.1 Criminals

Criminal hackers are very dangerous because of their newfound ability to work together and to leverage high levels of education. Unfortunately, as will be discussed in future chapters, criminals are not the "lone wolves" of the traditional hacking scene. Instead, they leverage their various skills in order to build more and better tools. It has long been suspected that various organized crime syndicates are involved in this, which makes the prospect even more frightening because they don't tend to give up.

5.2.2 Industrial Spies

Industrial espionage has been going on since industry began, but the new era of technology means those wishing to gain access to information have more and more opportunities. As will be discussed in Chapter 12, social engineering is a very effective technique used to trick an organization's employees to provide information on proprietary projects or even on people for use in short-cutting the research and development process or in enabling identity theft.

5.2.3 Ideologues

In a world of political moderates, the ability of people to affect change or at least gain publicity for their deeply-held beliefs strictly through their motivation to do so is astounding. Many protestors, such as those opposing western-style economic policies in developing countries, have been able to hack into sites to post their messages of protest, as well as being able to coordinate their protests over the Web, without meeting face-to-face.

5.2.4 Insiders

The threat of an insider abusing privilege is a major concern, as these people have been deemed as trustworthy by the organization in the past and have been granted access to the organization's networks. Unfortunately, when these employees become unhappy with their lot in life with the organization, an easy way for them to lash out is to abuse privilege or to commit a crime from within the walls of the organization itself.

5.2.5 Script Kiddies

Script kiddies are an annoyance but have the ability to cause real damage. This type of hacker is someone who is unable to or chooses not to develop their own exploits, but rather downloads them from the web and deploys them "out of the box."

5.3 The Paths to Intrusion

There are several "attack vectors" a hacker may use to penetrate an organization's networks.

First, they may simply walk into the target facility. As will be covered in the chapter on Physical Security, this type of intruder is often able to walk into a facility without arousing suspicion, such as through following someone through a door requiring an access card or key to get through. They will then walk up to an unoccupied and unlocked workstation and access the network.

Second, they could attempt to penetrate the network through a dial-up network. Old techniques included "wardialing," which is simply dialing numbers until a modem is reached. The attacker then attempts their exploit.

Third, wireless networks may be attacked. Wireless security is still relatively immature, and as such is comparatively easy to exploit. A measure of prevention against this is to deploy a Virtual Private Network (VPN) to control access to the organization's sensitive information. The trade-off, that someone is able to check their web email for free, is trivial.

Finally, the Internet is the primary vector. Not a month goes by without a new web browser exploit being developed and a patch to correct the problem released, it seems.

5.4 Malware

There are several types of computer programs used to attack systems, known collectively as "malware." Some examples are discussed below:

5.4.1 Viruses

A virus is a computer program that replicates itself from computer to computer and attacks each system it inhabits. As Strebe (2004) notes, there are two different operations:

- Propagation code, which is how the virus replicates itself, and
- Attack code, which performs the exploit.

If you have ever received a spam email from the email account of someone you know then your acquaintance has been the subject of an email virus attack, in which the attacker was able to exploit a hole in an email application and use the address book to send spam to all email addresses in the person's contact list.

5.4.2 Worms

While viruses require human actions, such as the opening of an email attachment, to spread, a worm spreads on its own. Worms usually have a Trojan Horse ("back door") program that allows the hacker to control a person's machine once it is installed.

The problem with worms is that they are very difficult if not impossible to detect, and should be defended against with supplemental protection, such as F-Secure.

5.4.3 Keyloggers

A keylogger is a program that, once installed, records a user's every keystroke. Needless to say, this is an extremely easy way for a hacker to gain a person's login information, as all characters typed on the keyboard will be visible to the intruder.

5.4.4 Rootkits

A rootkit, originally a set of Unix functionalities that provided the user with administrator-level access, has become a hacker tool. Anything that grants administrator-level control has a large potential to be exploited, and the real problem with a rootkit is that while an exploit may still be prevented from infecting a machine it is difficult to remove all traces of it from the system.

5.5 Conclusion

This chapter has described briefly the type of people who typically attempt to penetrate an organization's networks, the attack vectors they tend to use to do it and some of the myriad types of malware they may use to do their damage or collect their information.

5.6 Questions for Discussion

What type of anti-virus protection does your organization use?

As a preview for the chapter on physical security, does your organization have a policy charging employees with the responsibility of politely but firmly challenging all unknown, unbadged and unescorted persons at your facility?

Has your organization ever been the victim of a successful attack? How was it accomplished? What steps were taken to protect from the attack being repeated? What damage did it do to the organization? What *could* it have done?

Chapter 6 Encryption

Chapter 6 Objective

This chapter will discuss at a high level encryption and its uses.

6.1 Introduction

As was mentioned in the last chapter and earlier in the book, IT connectivity allows organizations to communicate around the world. Unfortunately, the ability of those wishing to "observe" what the organizations are doing seems to be running slightly ahead of the ability to stop them from doing so. An answer to this dilemma is encryption, which in essence "scrambles" the messages being sent over networks, rendering them unreadable.

6.2 The Information Sent Over Networks

Tyson (2006) notes that there is significant information that often travels over networks that we would not like to share with others, such as:

- Credit card information,
- Social Security numbers,
- Private (intimate, business) correspondence,
- Personal details, such as the names of family members and personal preferences, and
- Bank account information.

To protect the information, encryption systems such as those discussed below may be employed.

6.3 Encryption

Encryption stems from cryptography, the art and science of encoding messages to render them unreadable to those without the key to decode them. Most systems are one of two types:

- Symmetric-key, or
- Public-key (ibid)

6.3.1 Symmetric-Key Encryption

For symmetric-key arrangements two computers are each given the necessary keys to encrypt and decrypt information traveling between the two machines. This is basically a "secret code" between the two machines. The disadvantage, obviously, is that this type of encryption does no good if both machines are not available.

6.3.2 Public-Key Encryption

Public-key encryption is a hybrid of private keys and public keys. The intended recipient of an encoded message provides the sender with a public key, which is known to everyone. The sender encodes the message with the public key and then sends it to the receiver. The receiver then uses their private key (known only to them) in combination with the public key to decode the message.

6.3.3 Digital Certification

"In order to perform public-key encryption on a large scale, such as a secure Web server might need, requires (a specific) approach. A digital certificate is...a bit of information that says that the Web server is trusted by an independent source, known as a certificate authority."(ibid) These authorities, such as VeriSign, are trusted authorities for verifying the authenticity of a sender's certificate.

Important: As will be discussed later in the book, "phishing" websites use fake certificate authority logos to trick unsuspecting users into believing the site is secured by encryption when it is in fact not.

6.3.4 Secure Sockets Layer (SSL)

One implementation most web users will be familiar with is Secure Sockets Layer (SSL), even though it may not be recognizable by name. Instead, the users will have seen URLs that don't begin with:

http://

but rather

https://

The "s", which stands for "secure," may be verified by the existence of a small padlock (which should appear to be locked) at the bottom right of the screen (another popular phishing tactic is to plant a fake padlock on the static part of the fake site).

6.4 Authentication

As is the case with logon information, in an encryption there is a requirement to authenticate that the person is who they claim to be. Authentication may be accomplished by:

- Password,
- Pass cards, which serve as a type of token, and
- Digital signatures.

Digital signatures, which rely on the Digital Signature Standard, derived from the Digital Signature Algorithm, are attached to a document when the author completes it. If the document is changed after the digital signature is completed, the signature will be shown to be invalid. (Tyson, 2006)

6.5 Conclusion

The amount and type of information traveling over networks today is massive and varied. While mostly secure, there is a large potential for financial reward that serves as a motivating factor for capturing one's financial or personal information, which means that it is necessary to take measures to protect oneself from the would-be thieves. Encryption is a strong tool to be used in keeping your information private.

6.6 Discussion Questions

What kind of information do you regularly send over the internet? How often? What could be done with that information if someone came into possession of it?

Does your employer mandate that you use encryption? How many websites (Time and Attendance, Expense Reporting) do you go to with the https:// beginning to the URL?

Chapter 7 Balanced Scorecard

Chapter Objectives

This chapter will discuss:
- The role of a balanced scorecard,
- The balanced scorecard's four views,
- It's relevance to the organization as a whole, and
- The data it requires for relevance.

7.1 Introduction to the Balanced Scorecard

In the drive to present the vast amount of data available to an organization and its suppliers, a method for displaying aggregated data as it relates to organizational strategy in an easily understandable format has come into prominence in recent years and has been adopted by many organizations. This method, known as the "balanced scorecard," was originally developed by Kaplan and Norton (1992) and displays an evaluation of how an organization is succeeding in meeting expectations for measures such as timeliness and quality. But this kind of measurement "has consequences far beyond reporting on the past. Measurement creates focus for the future and communicates important messages to all organizational units and employees." (Kaplan and Norton, 2001) A balanced scorecard's primary function is to link an organization's strategy goals to quantifiable measures to indicate to the user the success or failure of the reporting entity or the organization as a whole relative to its (ideally) clearly stated goals. (Moshonas, 2003)

7.1.1 The Balanced Scorecard's Views

There are four views for a balanced scorecard (Kaplan and Norton, 2001b):

- Financial- "the strategy for growth, profitability, and risk viewed from the perspective of the shareholder.
- Customer- "the strategy for creating value and differentiation from the perspective of the customer.
- Internal Business Processes- "the strategic priorities for various business processes that create customer and shareholder satisfaction, and
- Learning and Growth- "the priorities to create a climate that supports organizational change, innovation, and growth."

For the financial perspective, the role of a properly defined "control environment," discussed in Chapter 18, is a key consideration. In order to know how the finances of an organization manifest, the processes the organization undertakes must be defined properly. This is especially true in the mergers and acquisitions arena, as disparate systems, many of which could be performing the same functions, will need to be integrated or surviving systems determined and those systems to be eliminated as a result of portfolio management. (Kaplan and Norton, 2006)

When considering the customer's perspective, the organization's ability to deliver value over a wide number of instances is realized. When different units of an organization have the same customer but treat them as entirely separate business relationships, there is no opportunity to explore if pricing may be adjusted for quantities purchased. This may not always be possible on shipping and handling, as geographically disparate locations could lead to the same cost to the shipper as before, but the total quantity ordered from the newly consolidated demand could qualify the customer for a discount. Efficiencies in shipping costs could also be passed on to the customer if items are sent to central locations in sufficient quantity. (ibid)

The process perspective seeks to discover how the organization can improve its internal process with its balanced scorecard. Often, various parts of an organization will perform the same business process separately. When consolidated, economies of scale are possible. (ibid) Kaplan and Norton's perspective of the Balanced Scorecard is shown in Figure 7.1 below.

7.1.2 How the Balanced Scorecard is Relevant to Each Employee

A balanced scorecard for each section of an organization demonstrates to each worker how their function "rolls up" to the next higher level and eventually how it contributes to the ultimate objective. (Gumbus and Lyons, 2002) Figure 7.2 shows visually the procession of information up and down the strategy map.

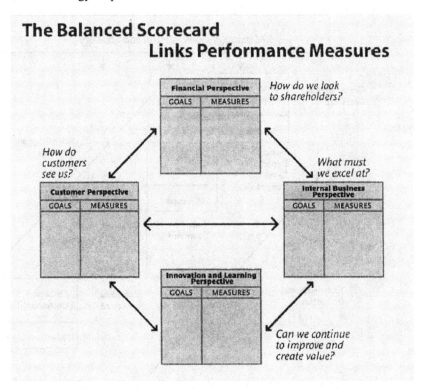

Figure 7.1 The Balanced Scorecard (Kaplan and Norton, 2005)

Niven (2003) describes the characteristics each measure should possess before it is included in a balanced scorecard:

- Linked to strategy- There should be a clear link in an organization's "strategy map" between a measure and each higher measure until eventually connecting with the ultimate strategic goal.

- Easy to understand- Each measure should be defined in a way that all competent employees will understand what the measure is and what is expected of them to meet the assigned level.
- Link in a chain of cause and effect- each measure should be applicable in all four views of the scorecard, as the views are not distinct but rather one of four "filters" to view information through.

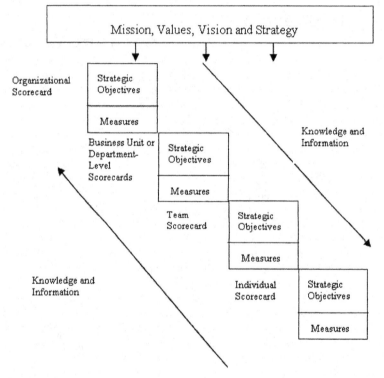

Figure 7.2 Knowledge Flowing in a Cascading Balanced Scorecard (adapted from: Niven, 2003)

- Updated frequently- Data gathered in real time may be used to update scorecards automatically. Not updating scorecards frequently enough can result in ineffective decision-making.
- Accessible- It is important to ensure that the type of data needed to truly tell if a system is succeeding is capturable.
- Average-cautious- Unusually high or low data points may result in an unrealistic viewpoint of the actual situation.

- Resistant to specific dates- Niven argues that a measure to complete a project by a certain date is more of an initiative and not appropriate for inclusion on a balanced scorecard.
- Quantitative- Yes/no responses, for example, are not quantitative measures. The percentage of reports received on time, however, would be considered quantitative. Many of the key measures will begin with "What percentage of..." "How many..." and "How long ago...", as these statements may be answered quantitatively.

7.1.3 Dysfunctional Processes

Niven also discusses the implications when a balanced scorecard creates a process that is dysfunctional. Niven uses an example of a "wasted food" measure that actually hurt a restaurant. To avoid waste, the cooks were ordered to not prepare any food until actually ordered by patrons beginning one hour before the kitchen closed. This led to longer wait times for food to be served and resulted in lost business, overwhelming the savings realized from reduced waste. An organization should take care to ensure their well-intentioned improvement does not result in an overall negative impact.

Instead, what managers should do is leverage the balanced scorecard by realizing first that "customers' concerns tend to fall into four categories: time, quality, performance and service, and cost," which links directly to Leibenstein's discussion of "X-inefficiency" in Chapter 16. To leverage the balanced scorecard properly, the general principals (goals) delineated by the scorecard must be translated into "specific measures." The measures must then be applied to the organization's business processes. (Kaplan and Norton, 2005) In each of the following chapters there is a section addressing the balanced scorecard as it applies to the chapter material.

7.2   How a Balanced Scorecard Succeeds

The major benefits of a balanced scorecard are discussed by Kaplan and Norton (2005) as a link to a senior executive effort to manage strategy within the organization. They focus on three areas of benefit:

- *Planning and Budgeting.* Because senior management tends to receive funding recommendations from the various sub-units of their organizations, the best way for those preparing the input to do the best job possible is to know the objectives of the organization from the "touchpoints" their part shares with others, both vertically and horizontally. In addition, they must be aware of cross-functional initiatives they share with other parts of the organization.

- ***Human Resource Alignment.*** Kaplan and Norton note that "no strategy can be effective unless the people who have to carry it out are motivated and trained to do so." (ibid) Specific methods of managerial communication and training are discussed in Chapters 16 and 17. When an organization's priorities change, human capital must either be trained to handle new responsibilities or new workers must be brought in. In both the U.S. private and public sectors the emphasis would be to first re-train the existing workforce if possible. In the private sector, however, it is much easier to exchange workers who are not succeeding in the new environment than it is in the public sector, a major source of inefficiency.

- ***Knowledge Management.*** The key motivation behind knowledge management (KM) is to share information and best practices throughout the organization. In many organizations, the ways in which one employee or section is succeeding are never known by the rest of the staff. Some organizations have assigned a Chief Knowledge Officer to transfer knowledge throughout the organization.

Important: An organization should be very hesitant to allow its employees to "self evaluate" when determining how well they are accomplishing their mission. The author has direct experience of this kind of situation.

In this particular work environment, a balanced scorecard regime had been established but results were, until very shortly before he changed projects, scores given by those charged to do the work while the person in charge of reporting to senior management, a person who worked very conscientiously to meet his responsibilities, was reporting what the workers wanted management to hear rather than objective fact.

In addition, the categories used on the balanced scorecard had long ceased to be relevant to what was actually going on in the organization. In the end, while a "box was checked," the data was 100% unreliable as it rolled up to senior management.

A final consideration in the balanced scorecard discussion is its data requirements. Data is a major concern in a modern organization, with applications in regulatory compliance and legal discovery in addition to being the "fuel" an organization creates and consumes in its daily operations. Kirschnick (2006) argues:

> **"For a BSC to be a success, all data sources need to provide up-to-date and consistent (single point of truth). This is the only way that a BSC can deliver a transparent and accurate flow of information for decision-making and (organization) controlling. However, most (organizations) do not currently have a uniform database in place."**

7.3   Conclusion

The balanced scorecard represents is a well-established and thorough methodology to link the functions an organization carries out in executing its business processes. By demonstrating how each function or group of functions "roll up" an organization all employees are able to see how their jobs benefit their workplace as a whole.

7.4   Discussion Questions

Think about your work. Do you rely on input from others to do your job? If yes, do you use the data as an entity unto itself (such as a credit score, or a bit of information that you use as a part of what you do), or do you take the information as an aggregation?

If any, what information do you pass on to your managers? What responsibilities do they have that your information helps them fulfill?

As a preview for later chapters, what information does senior management share with you about your role in the organization? If you are a senior manager, what do you do to ensure all employees understand to the best of their abilities their role in what the organization is trying to accomplish?

Chapter 8 Sarbanes-Oxley

Chapter Objectives

This chapter will discuss:
- How the internet scandals of the late 1990s and early 2000s led to Sarbanes-Oxley (SOX),
- What SOX is;
- The consequences of violating SOX,
- Risk management and data auditing as a key to gaining SOX compliance,
- Due diligence with members of the company's extended enterprise,
- Document retention, and
- The cost of compliance and possible mid-course corrections for outside auditors.

8.1 Scandal Leads to Regulation

With the massive amounts of fraud in the U.S. during the Internet boom, of which the Enron scandal is the most obvious case in point, political pressure was exerted on politicians to ensure this kind of scandal would not occur in the future. The result was the Sarbanes-Oxley Act of 2002 (SOX), which mandates financial accountability for publicly traded companies. This chapter describes the law and then discusses its relevance to compliance and an organization's business objectives as a whole.

8.2 SOX Described

SOX, while brief, established a major financial responsibility on organizations, especially their senior executives. Wagner and Dittmar (2006) highlight three sections of the statute:

- Section 302- Corporate Responsibility for Financial Reports. This section requires CEOs and CFOs personally attest to the accuracy of all financial statements and disclosures made by the company.

- Section 906- Corporate Responsibility for Financial Reports. This section requires CEOs and CFOs to affirm that submitted reports comply with government reporting requirements with substantial penalties for failing to do so.

- Section 404- This section, the one most relevant to this book, requires a yearly audit to evaluate the internal controls in place to ensure financial reporting is accurate. This is what Dittmar and Wagner (ibid) refer to as a "control environment." They summarize the section as follows:

"This section calls for an annual evaluation of internal controls and procedures for financial reporting. Like Section 302, Section 404 requires CEOs and CFOs to periodically assess and vouch for their effectiveness.

"Section 404 also obliges companies to include an internal-control report in their annual report. Although the SEC has not spelled out all of the elements of the internal-control report, it has indicated that the document should contain the following:

"- a statement acknowledging responsibility for establishing and maintaining adequate internal control over financial reporting

"- a statement identifying the internal-control framework used to evaluate the effectiveness of internal control over financial reporting

"- an assessment of the effectiveness of the company's internal control over financial reporting as of the end of the most recent fiscal year

"- disclosure of any material weaknesses in the company's internal control over financial reporting (if any material weaknesses exist, then internal control over financial reporting is deemed ineffective)

"- a statement that the independent auditor has issued a report on the company's assessment of internal control over financial reporting

"In addition, Section 404 requires a company's external auditor to examine and report on management's assessment of internal controls, as well as the effectiveness of the controls themselves." (Wagner and Dittmar, 2006)

Important: This internal control regime, which Wagner and Dittmar term a "control environment," is discussed in more detail in Chapter 18.

8.2.1 The Consequences of Violating SOX

While how the enforcement of SOX will evolve has not yet become apparent, what is clear is that the intent of the U.S. government is to go to great lengths to ensure that investors in publicly traded companies are able to base their decisions on fully truthful information. The government has developed a "culpability score" for a company alleged to have violated part of the statute. (Imperato, 2005) Critical aspects of the score are:

- "Timely and complete disclosure"- Once a potential violation is found, it may be counted against a corporation if they do not cooperate quickly and completely.
- "The corporation's willingness to implicate those responsible even if they are top management.
- "The corporation's cooperation in making witnesses available to the government and to encourage witness honesty and full disclosure, and
- "The disclosure of the results of the corporation's own internal investigation so that the facts and scope of the misconduct can be fully known to the government, even if this requires waiver of the attorney-client and/or work product privileges."

In addition to the responsibilities of companies, individuals have their own ways of being evaluated for punishment or even disqualification from positions of financial responsibility in public companies. Crowe and Ca-navan (2005) note that the standards include:

- "The egregiousness of the violations,
- "Whether the actor is a 'repeat offender,'
- "The person's position in the company when the violation oc-curred,
- "The individual's degree of 'scienter' that is, the degree to which an actor intends to deceive,
- "The person's economic stake and (most important)
- "The likelihood of reoccurrence."

8.2.2 Managing Risk to Avoid Violating SOX

To be compliant with SOX, a company must establish an environment in which, through its control of its business processes, it manages the risk of fraud or malfeasance being committed. Risk management is a very different situation than a compliance regime in which an organization must adhere to specific standards, as is the case with, for example, auditing requirements for the U.S. Department of Defense (DOD). In the DOD, and the U.S. government in general, being "compliant" means to adhere to a uniform standard and to perform a function in a specific way. In the private sector, however, compliance may be achieved in any number of ways, as long as the effectiveness of the controls is established with an external auditor.

The first step in determining how to be compliant with any regime is to ask the question "How could this organization become at risk of prosecution for violating SOX? What is it that we do and how we do it that could possibly expose us?" This risk assessment can be conducted in a "risk times impact" formula. In this calculation, the potential negative consequences to the company of a certain occurrence is multiplied by the risk of that event happening. If, for example, there is a 1% chance of unauthorized disclosure happening with every transaction, and 300 transactions occur each day, then on an average day three unauthorized disclosures will be made! If the minimum damage caused by disclosure is zero, but the maximum is $10,000, then on the worst day possible $30,000 worth of damage will be done to the company.

Engle (2005) states that "once the risk assessment is performed, the enterprise should identify and document the current control environment, which includes the policies, procedures, and internal controls operating within the company that address identified risks. Controls might include the board of directors' approval of management's strategic plan and annual budgets, quarterly reviews of financial results, or third-party assessments of financial reporting processes by an independent auditor."

> **Important:** It is essential that an organization know how its business processes are accomplished in today's environment. No longer is a senior executive able to disavow knowledge of how their company's financial statements came to be.

A key case in point in compliance comes in access to an organization's data. Because of an increasing demand for complete and accurate reports in "real time," more reliance is being placed on individual employees inputting information into IT systems which is then made available as itself or as a part of a "rolled up" report for management, perhaps through a Service Oriented Architecture (SOA), which allows anyone with the proper permissions to access information from anywhere within an extended enterprise.

In order for the reports to be valid, however, the information in the system must be accurate and only accessed or changed by authorized users. This requires that who is authorized to add, edit and delete data into systems must be defined. The only way to properly establish these roles is through a thorough understanding of the organization's business processes to know who person or which job is the "single source of truth" for each piece of data going into the system and the level of permissions they need to be able to do their job.

Simply documenting a business process and establishing a policy is not in and of itself sufficient. As Benanto (2005) argues, however, knowing the roles is not enough, as "even authorized users will sometimes access data inappropriately, deliberately or accidentally. (Also), flaws in policy and implementation can introduce vulnerability, enabling unintended data access or changes." In addition to the policies and procedures, a reliable audit process to ensure unauthorized changes or accesses have not occurred is also required. Rhinehart (in Lamont, 2005) notes that compliance "is an ongoing effort, and they need to figure out ways to reduce the costs...There is a stated requirement to map out and test processes for internal controls, but in addition, there is a burden of proof to demonstrate that the process was followed."

> **Important:** While SOX compliance is a major undertaking and is very complex, note the key elements of the process: defining business processes, the organizations and people involved, and the data elements generated or used by the organization in executing its business processes. These elements would, for example, provide the documentation required to form the baseline for transitioning to a next-generation IT strategy, such as a Service-Oriented Architecture.

Benanto (2005) provides several technical capabilities required for "an effective solution providing data access accountability":

- Capture Data Access- The system must be built in a way that whenever data is accessed, changed or viewed the data and the user are logged.
- Capture Structural Changes- The system must be built in a way that when permissions of users are changed or when the schema (structure) of the data is changed the changes are noted.
- Manage Captured Information- Information generated or captured by systems should be consolidated into a single repository.
- Centralize Configuration and Management of All Servers- Auditing should be straightforward to configure across the entire universe of involved systems.
- Flexible Information Access- Auditors should be able to use the available information in several different ways to facilitate their analysis.
- Produce Reports- A report function (such as that available in the Enterprise Architecture tool ARIS from IDS-Scheer) is a key functionality in order to provide analytical results in a form understandable to executives who are intelligent but untrained in the specific application without forcing the analyst to spend significant amounts of time "translating" the output so non-technical people can use it.

8.2.3 Due Diligence with Offsite Partners

In the modern business world, organizations are compelled to grant access to business data and even internal systems to partners or service providers. This, however, does nothing to lessen a company's SOX compliance burden. Bednarz (2005) notes that "due diligence to section 404 means looking into conditions at outsourcing and hosting providers' sites, where sensitive corporate data might be accessible, processed or stored."

The mechanism with which to establish with auditors that the outside organization has adequate controls over its own processes is the Statement on Auditing Standards (SAS) 70 report, a standard established by the American Institute of Certified Public Accountants. While there is some lack of clarity over when a SAS 70 is required, the general rule should be that when in doubt the report should be demanded of the partner. In addition, there is no single "SAS 70" format, which means they are defined by individual organizations and as such completing a SAS 70 would not be sufficient in and of itself to satisfy SOX auditors. (ibid)

Important: SAS 70 reports have been deemed important enough by Yankee Candle's CFO that if a major partner does not produce a SAS 70 report that the company will terminate the relationship. (Wagner and Dittmar, 2006)

8.2.4 Document Retention

During the Enron scandal news coverage in the U.S., a key aspect was the decision to destroy documents material to the discovery/investigative process. In light of the current regulatory environment Isaza (2005) listed some guidelines for a legally valid document retention policy.

First, there must be a "clear, written document retention policy and schedules that meet its business needs and are fully endorsed by management. The policy should define when, where, and by whom records are required by law, contract or value to the company are routed to appropriate archives and stipulate records no longer required are properly destroyed. Companies must also specify the means of destruction."

Second, the company must ensure the policy is properly communicated and that it is followed in a way that can be established with outside parties.

Third, "companies must enact administrative procedures that will immediately stop the routine destruction of records when and if they become the subject of corporate governance, regulatory or legal concerns."

Finally, "companies must guide and train all employees on how prepare effective, accurate records." (ibid)

8.2.5 Compliance is Costly

The method the SEC has chosen for companies to gain SOX certification is through an audit performed by an independent outside accounting company. The cost of these audits has been more than 20 times higher than was originally estimated by regulators. In fact, not all costs are associated with the actual audit, but could come from a requirement to purchase new IT systems so business processes may be audited sufficiently to prevent abuse. Even more, not all costs of the process are direct, but are also indirect, such as the opportunity costs of other work that could have been accomplished had it not been for the SOX requirement, as well as the cost of training employees how to conduct business in a compliant manner. (Hagenbaugh and Krantz, 2005).

8.2.6 Mid-Course Corrections?

As will be discussed in Chapter 17, a willingness to make mid-course corrections in a policy is an essential part of ensuring a process realizes its intended goals in the most efficient way possible. The zealousness of some auditors has become a source of complaints by companies subjected to what they feel are overly harsh requirements. For example, a company noted that a workday's worth of effort was required to prepare the documentation needed to be allowed to change a single line of code in their inventory systems. All this effort was justified by a third-party auditor as necessary for SOX compliance. (Frauenhaim, 2005)

In response to this and many other complaints, the SEC and the Public Company Accounting Oversight Board (PCAOB, pronounced "peek-a-boo") found that auditors had been "overly cautious" and "mechanical" in their approaches and that they should exercise more professional judgment when determining the legitimacy of a practice and avoid a "one size fits all" perspective. (Solomon and Gullapalli, 2005)

The compliance environment in the U.S. is a constant "tug of war" between companies and government. With the Enron debacle still fresh in the electorate's memory, though, it is most probable that financial auditing requirements will not be weakened substantially for some time if at all.

8.3 Applying the Balanced Scorecard to SOX

The goals and their measures in establishing a reference SOX balanced scorecard are:

Goal: Ensure SOX is understood by senior management.
- The organization's legal department understands SOX-
  - o How much experience does the company's legal department have with SOX compliance?
  - o If the current SOX compliance lawyers were to leave, how would the company go about replacing them? Would someone within the company be able to step in, or would an outsider need to be hired?
- Senior management is educated about SOX and its requirements-
  - o How long has it been since senior management was certified as to SOX requirements?
  - o How long has it been since senior management reviewed SOX compliance policies?

Goal: Lessen the risk of a SOX violation
- Understand the company's business processes-
  - o When did the company last study its workforce to determine how each worker accomplishes their jobs?
  - o How long has it been since the last time the company ascertained how each position fits into the company as a whole?
- Understand the company's extended enterprise-
  - o How long has it been since the company last studied its relationships with the members of its extended enterprise?
- Perform risk assessment regarding the opportunities for SOX violations to occur-
  - o How long has it been since each business process was analyzed to determine potential areas of risk for SOX violations?
- Perform data audits to be provided to independent analysts-
  - o How long has it been since the permissions and physical structures associated with data in the company's IT systems been documented and analyzed?
  - o How often are data audits routinely performed to ascertain whether employees are abusing their privileges or if data

is being accessed by those without permission? How long
ago was the last such audit?

- Perform due diligence with outside parties-
  - o Has the outside party established its ability to control sen-
    sitive company information adequately, such as through
    providing a satisfactory SAS 70 report? How long ago
    was the last submission?
- Establish a document retention plan-
  - o Have all document retention requirements been developed
    and approved by independent auditors? How long ago
    was this approval last received?
  - o Have all relevant employees been verifiably trained as to
    the document retention policy? How current is their train-
    ing?
  - o Are internal audits performed regularly to ensure the
    document retention policy is being followed? How long
    ago was the last such audit?

8.4 Conclusion

Compliance with any regulation is difficult and is often seen as a barrier
to actually being able to accomplish an organization's mission. For SOX,
this has been the case, as shown by the complaints regarding the expense
and time burdens foisted on the companies by auditors. While the government has conceded that the auditors have been overzealous in some instances, there is certainly no indication that government oversight of corporate reporting will diminish any time soon. As will be discussed in
Chapter 18, there are several benefits to be gained from completing a SOX
audit successfully.

8.5 Discussion Questions

Aside from Sarbanes-Oxley, which laws and regulations apply to your
organization as well? Are there any which were designed especially for
organizations in your sector?

Think about your daily job. If you wanted to, how easy would it be to
gain access to data to which you are not entitled? Are you able to access
systems that contain sensitive or personal data? If you're not able to access the information yourself, do you have a "source" in the organization
willing to provide you with information when you request it?

Do you in your daily job interact with outside organizations which have access to sensitive data from your organization? What type of data do they see (financial, technical, personal)? What could someone who had that information potentially do with it if they wanted to?

Have you ever been asked to document the processes you perform as you do your job? If yes, did they explain why?

Have you ever been trained as to which documents should be retained and for how long?

Chapter 9 Physical Security

Chapter Objectives

This chapter will discuss:
- How to decide on where to locate your organization's IT equipment,
- Some suggested ways employee identification may be accomplished to distinguish among various levels of access,
- How to handle an outgoing employee's physical access while they are transitioning out of the organization,
- How to handle visitors to the organization's facilities, and
- How the balanced scorecard for physical security could look at a high level.

9.1   Physical Security- Easily Overlooked

In today's world, the "cops and robbers" game of those trying to extract information from an organization versus those trying to prevent it is normally seen as a purely technological battle. While technology does indeed play a dominating role in the discipline, and IT managers likely see physical security as a mundane detail that is appropriately handled by operations, this chapter is included because it is absolutely critical for all connected with protecting an organizations' assets to understand that penetration attempts occur from many different angles. This chapter, the social engineering section and the discussion on what influences an employee's behavior while on the job are especially important in dealing with the human element of security. When the French were convinced they were going to be invaded during World War II, they built what they thought was an impenetrable barrier of firepower known as the "Maginot Line". As it turned out, however, the invading force attacked from another direction. Because the Maginot Line wasn't mobile, the defense was pointed in the wrong direction and rendered useless. This serves as a good analogy for IT security, in that the best defense against attack from one direction, over the network, is useless if the penetration comes from "behind the firewall".

9.2   Where to Locate Computer Equipment

Almost every organization will at some point be forced to deal with a disaster brought on by fire, water, or electrical surge. Policies for backup and disaster recovery are covered elsewhere, so the discussion here will focus solely on the optimal location for the actual IT equipment. Key factors to consider when making this decision are:

- How much control do you have over the layout of your space?
- Where are candidate sites relative to external entrances?
- To what extent is the environment for the site controllable?

How Much Control Do You Have Over the Layout of Your Space?

For most companies, their real estate will be leased rather than owned, which will limit the options on how the space containing the IT equipment will be set up.

Are there "drop" ceilings? Drop ceilings are ceilings for a room that purposefully create space between the true ceiling and that of the working area by placing a structure, usually a metal grid on which foam panels are laid, with enough space for workers to run wire to offices from the server room without it being seen in the regular working area. Access is covered in another part of this chapter, but if there are drop ceilings adequate care should be taken to ensure that someone with a ladder and some agility will not be able to remove one or two ceiling panels and bypass the access door to the server room without at least an alarm being triggered.

Are the floors raised? Another way to enable wire to be run is by the opposite technique of a drop ceiling, a raised floor. This option is somewhat less flexible, in that to change a wiring configuration carpet, at the very least, will need to be moved aside, but for what is likely to be a permanent setup it works very well. A telltale sign of a raised floor is a drumlike sound whenever a person weighing over 180 pounds (about 82 kilograms) walks by while wearing dress shoes.

How much space is available in the server room? This factor is becoming less and less critical now that space-saving hardware such as blade servers are available, but knowing how much space one has to work with allows management to make decisions with physical space constraints in mind.

Where are Candidate Server Room Sites Relative to External Entrances?

In many leased locations, there will often be only one or two places in which it makes sense to locate a dedicated server room. When there is a choice, the room will not be one with external windows, as those will be used for offices, and will not be "on the border" with another organization's office space or common area, such as the hallway to the restrooms or the elevator lobby. Should it be necessary to locate the server room close to uncontrolled space, the same precautions for triggering alarms as discussed above should be taken.

Another factor to consider is how much time it would take a thief to reach the server room, or a room where proprietary information is stored, gain access and secure the desired items, and leave the scene.

What is the procedure and response time for your security company and for your organization when an alarm is activated? The traditional contract security company in the U.S. will have a contact number to call as soon as an alarm is activated. Be certain to know the standard procedure the security company follows when an alarm goes off. Do they contact the police immediately, or do they wait for the company's point of contact to instruct them to do so? Does this vary based on the time of day? What if the point of contact is traveling or is otherwise unavailable? Does the security company have several different numbers to call if the main point of contact doesn't respond? Are you able to change who is to be called anytime you wish? Most important, how quickly do these steps happen? If the intruders know the physical location of their target and are proficient, they could use the "smash and grab" technique, in which they judge they could get away without being caught even if they set off an alarm the second they begin their operation. This scenario is a race against time, as the intruders try to leave the scene before the police respond. It may even help for you to determine how a robbery would likely happen and time how long it would take for someone to access the target equipment, secure it and exit the facility.

What was just described may seem to be more drastic than would likely occur, but when one weighs the impact of the loss of years or perhaps even decades of effort to a thief's concerted effort the extra effort is worth the trouble. In addition, as discussed elsewhere, rigorous backup and disaster recovery policies should be implemented.

> **Important: Know the procedure your security company follows when an alarm is set off and have your own internal procedure in place to react!**

To What Extent is the Environment for the Site Controllable?

Another key consideration in placing the server room is the ability to control the climate of that room individually. Because of the heat generated by several machines operating at the same time and IT equipment's sensitivity to heat, this room must be kept at a significantly lower temperature than the areas occupied by employees. Is there a thermostat specifically for the server room? If the temperature for an area must be kept low, care must be taken to ensure employees who can operate in lower temperatures occupy the offices. Remember, some people are able to tolerate lower temperatures better than others!

9.3   Employee Identification Procedures

Once an organization reaches the size (usually about fifty employees) where everyone does not know everyone else by sight or must ensure its facility is secure to comply with various secure facility requirements it will be necessary to issue employee identification (ID) cards. The key question at this point becomes: How detailed and expensive does the ID need to be? As with most things, the more complex and useful the ID the more expensive it is to produce. With that in mind, the following discussion addresses badge design, use and limitations.

9.3.1   Badge Data Elements

As the familiar saying goes, a picture is worth a thousand words. A badge is in essence a picture communicating to others the levels of access and critical characteristics of a person's role within an organization.

> **Important: Err on the side of inclusion when designing a badge if the purpose of the program is to do anything more than to comply with minimum requirements. Several design features will be discussed below; the more features included means the more utility the badges will have.**

Required Elements

When designing a company badge, the following items should always be included:

The employee's full first and last names. This is the most obvious bit of information to be included, but care should be taken when deciding whether to allow for nicknames or abbreviations to be used. If, for example, the ID is intended for use as a second form of identification it would be necessary for the employee's full name to be used rather than a nickname. Also, if an employee changes their name after, for example, getting married, it would be necessary to update the badge to reflect this change.

A recent picture. As silly as this may seem, the ability of a new security officer or employee to be able to verify that the person representing themselves as a member of the organization is critical. In fact, employees should be trained to ask another employee or the security officer to verify a person's identity should there be any doubt whatsoever, as once information is disclosed, it's in the open forever. While it is likely not necessary to update an ID every time someone changes their hair color, it would be wise to have IDs expire every two or three years and that the ID's picture be retaken when reissued.

Expiration date. In order to prevent a former employee or an impersonator from using an old ID to gain access to a facility, the badge's expiration date should be featured prominently.

> **Important:** **Be certain the picture and font size on the badge is large enough for these required elements to be read by a normally sighted person at a socially acceptable distance. If the printing is too small, people may be hesitant to inspect the badges closely enough for fear of being impolite.**

Optional Elements

The following features may also be included on an employee's badge but might not need to be readable from a distance:

Hologram. This feature adds cost, but is a strong way of establishing the authenticity of an ID. Holograms are much more difficult to forge, but to use a generally available hologram design could actually prove to be more of a liability than a benefit, as the perception of security provided by having a hologram could make the organization less vigilant as a whole, allowing an intruder to gain access when they would otherwise have been challenged.

Home office. Once an organization opens more than one office or has employees who work offsite, colleagues may not meet for extended periods of time or at all. As seen in the discussion on social engineering, a prime technique for an attacker to gain access to information or a facility is by posing as an employee from another part of the facility. If the employee's badge notes their base of operations, any need to verify their bona fides would be resolved with a call to their office's security officer.

9.3.2 Badge Design

Aside from that conveyed by words, badge design elements may be used to communicate levels of access and other information:

Badge Color. The color of a badge may be used to indicate several elements, such as native/non-native citizenship or government employee/contractor.

Important: The badge's primary color should be used to communicate the most important piece of information to your organization outside of the required elements addressed earlier. If, for example, citizenship is paramount, the badge color should signify this element. If clearance level is most important, it should communicate that element.

Picture Border. Additionally, a border around the employee's picture may be used to give information. Perhaps a particular color of border denotes the employee has unescorted access to a restricted part of the building.

Symbols. A common way to denote an employee's access level, such as security clearance, is through the use of symbols on the badge. In the U.S. a Secret, Top Secret and clearances above Top Secret may be indicated by one and two or more symbols on the badge. Another way to accomplish the same objective is to use different symbols for different clearances.

9.3.3   Other Badging Considerations

A few other key considerations for a badge's use should also be noted:

Is the employee ID also the card that grants access to the facility?
Organizations who lease their facilities will often have the security provided by a company under contract to the property management firm in charge of operating the building, which will necessitate using a separate card or key to access the facility. When this happens, an employee who has had their access card stolen will be able to show valid ID with their employee badge and will be able to gain access to the facility through being allowed in by the receptionist or fellow workers. An employee forgetting their access card is not unusual, and the employee's assurance that it was simply left in a jacket pocket or on the nightstand should not cause concern, but it is advisable that an employee who does not have their card should have that fact reported to the facility security officer and that employee should be required to show the receptionist or the security officer the next time they are in the office that they do in fact still have the card. This step is very simple and reasonable, and makes it more likely a stolen card will be deactivated before it is used by unauthorized individuals.

For facilities where a badge is also used as an access card, employees should be guided to report a lost or stolen badge as soon as possible. When an employee forgets their ID, the receptionist should issue them a temporary badge and report the issuance to the facility's security officer. For badges that are forgotten or lost, automatic deactivation is a step to be considered if the bearer would have access to the facility after work hours during a time in which critical information may be vulnerable.

Are separate badges or special codes required for access to the server room? In many organizations only those from the IT department and senior management are allowed access to server rooms, which is a logical step given that a regular employee must only use the services provided by the hardware.

9.4   Employees Transitioning Out of the Organization

When an employee resigns, is laid off or terminated, the level of access they should retain during their transition is an important consideration. Non-disclosure agreements serve as a legal deterrent to misbehavior, but there are times when an employee's bitterness with the organization has caused them to take proprietary information with them or provide it to other parties, such as their future employers, before their access was cut off. While legal maneuvers and punishments are available to mitigate the damage done through this means, it is much better to avoid the information leaving the organization in the first place. Each case is different and should be treated as such while preserving the organization's right to keep its intellectual property safe.

The first matter to consider is, if possible, access to sensitive information should be restricted. Needless to say, an employee on their way out of the organization should no longer be allowed to work on proposals or anything in which private company information is involved, but how does that translate to the work products for their and other projects? Are an individual's access privileges able to be changed to allow them access to their remaining job but not to internal folders? If not, should the employee's usage be subjected to an additional level of monitoring? If the employee has resigned, a decision on whether an audit of their activity in the time leading up to their giving notice is desired. If the employee has been laid off or terminated, their access should be cut off as quickly as possible.

The other issue to be discussed here is collecting any information technology devices issued to the employee by the company. Several questions should be taken into account when considering how the turn-in will proceed:

Is there a policy describing the allowable use company-provided equipment? The author is not a lawyer, but in the absence of a policy stating that an employee must use the equipment solely for company business it is easy to assume that there could possibly be implications as to an organization's ability to demand it immediately upon notice of the employee's departure. Personal information and non-company-related projects could be stored on the computer and could potentially be used as justification for delaying turning in the equipment. Should a policy be enacted that upon an employee leaving the organization their equipment will be expected immediately with no expectation that any personal data will be returned to the employee, then the organization would likely be in much more firm standing.

Is there a specific policy delineating the turn-in procedure? Based on what is allowable personal use of company-provided equipment, the equipment turn-in procedure should accommodate the legitimate expectations of the outgoing employee while maintaining the organization's right to protect its intellectual property. The best way for the organization to protect itself is to require the equipment to be given to the company when notification is given, which enables management to control access to its internal drives as thoroughly as possible. One way to balance the employee's expectation of having personal files returned to them will be to designate a specific folder within which the employee keeps personal items. After the equipment has been returned to the organization, the personal folder may be inspected and all personal folders and files returned to the employee. Again, if there is any doubt consult an attorney to enact the policy that best fits your needs.

Has or will an exit interview be conducted? Exit interviews are of varying utility to an organization. In many industries, the community is not very large and the major players know each other. Because the person in transition will most likely not want to "burn bridges" through criticizing the organization or specific people in the organization and thus risk their being spoken of in negative terms to potential employers or to sufficiently alienate their current employer that they would not be hired back should the opportunity arise, they will likely temper their comments and simply explain that they felt it was time to go in a new direction or that they want to be able to spend more time with their family. While these could, of course, be the actual reasons a person would voluntarily decide to leave an organization it is unlikely they would do so unless they felt in some way unsatisfied with their situation. While difficult and sometimes embarrassing to hear, employees on their way out of an organization should be encouraged to share their true feelings. Promises the comments will not be shared are given as a matter of course, but whether the employee will believe it depends on how they have been treated during their time with the organization and on how they have seen other employees who have left referred to after they are gone.

9.5 Visitor Policy

Another key consideration in an organization's physical security is how visitors to the facility are handled. For some U.S. government- or contractor-run facilities, it is necessary to file a Visitor Authorization Letter before access may be permitted. In the private sector, access to a specific building or area may require pre-screening before a visitor is permitted to enter. Consult government or corporate security professionals for the exact requirements for a Visit Authorization Letter, but the following information will generally be required:

- **Full Legal Name-** For a facility requiring this level of pre-screening, even a middle initial is insufficient.
- **Organization-** Knowledge of which entity the potential visitor is representing can play a vital role in deciding whether or not to grant them access to the facility.
- **Social Security Number-** This is needed to enable the security office to conduct a background check on the individual if deemed necessary. The applicant should be made aware that the organization to be visited reserves the right to perform a background check on all potential visitors at its sole discretion.
- **Citizenship-** In some circumstances citizens of countries other than that represented by the hosting facility may not be permitted or may require a different procedure for gaining access.
- **Internal Point of Contact-** This is the name and extension of the person responsible for the visitor for the duration of their stay at the facility.
- **Purpose of Visit-** This helps establish the requirement for the visit as well as to aid in any investigation resulting from suspicious activity.
- **Length of Visit-** Stays range from less than an hour to multiple weeks. Is there a specific threshold for an authorization letter to be required? Is there a maximum amount of time a visitor is allowed to stay without interruption?
- **Criminal Record Check Complete?-** For a government facility, it may be required that the applicant have had a criminal background check run. If the applicant has a Common Access Card (CAC) which is issued by the U.S. Department of Defense, for example, a criminal record background check is part of the routine process in obtaining the card.

For a commercial facility, not all of the above elements may be required, but care should be taken to determine the bona fides of the potential visitor if they are requesting access to an area that would potentially give them access to "the crown jewels."

9.5.1 Visitor Sign-In Sheet

A strongly suggested method of maintaining control over access to your organization's facility is to require all visitors to sign in, including all badged employees who have forgotten their badges that day. The information required to be issued a visitor's badge is similar to that needed for a Visit Authorization Letter to be approved, but has a few additional elements:

- **Name**
- **Organization**
- **Contact Number**
- **Host Organization Point of Contact and Phone Number**
- **Time in-** This allows for the organization to audit who was in the facility should it become necessary to investigate suspicious activity.
- **Badge Number-** This information is to be filled out by the security officer issuing the badge. A key consideration here is whether an escort is required for the visitor no matter where they are in the facility. Badges should indicate clearly that the person is a visitor and whether or not an escort is required.

Time Out- Upon return of the visitor's badge, the security officer should fill in the time the visitor exited the facility. Many organizations are less stringent with this requirement than with the others, but for full auditability it is best to know the time all visitors have exited the facility.

9.5.2 Controlled Items

A controlled item is any device that may be used to capture or record information against the wishes of the host organization. With the explosion of multi-functional information devices available in the consumer market, it is a constant challenge for security to stop controlled items from entering a facility. A few examples of controlled items are discussed below:

- **Laptops-** If a person shows up for a meeting in the U.S. without a laptop, they almost assuredly forgot it or intentionally left it behind. In addition to most modern laptops having the ability to copy compact disks, download information from USB ("flash" or "thumb") drives and to record sound without the others in the meeting knowing they are being recorded, care must be taken to decide if outside laptops are going to be allowed in the facility. If they are, a form declaring all controlled items to the facility's security office should be required.

- **Digital Cameras-** While these devices are not frequently carried for business purposes, they are able to capture the whiteboard in a conference room in an instant. If the board happens to contain strategic information, such as a plan for a new product or a proposal the attacker's organization may have an interest in, that information is now in their hands. Many digital cameras also have the ability to record video as well, so not hearing a click and a flash doesn't mean you're not being recorded. Of particular concern is the inclusion of digital cameras in cell phones and personal data assistants (PDAs). Many facilities prohibit any device capable of taking pictures, which makes it inconvenient for visitors to maintain contact with their offices while visiting these facilities.
- **Portable Drives-** Easily concealed in a pocket or secreted in a larger, innocent-looking item and with storage capacities of 1GB and more, these drives, usually connecting through a USB port, epitomize convenience and the ability to quickly download information without anyone knowing until audit logs are checked. Some government facilities disable USB drives on their computers in response. As an example of the stealthy nature of the portable drive, they don't always come in forms that we naturally associate with a portable drive. In fact, portable music players are nothing more than portable drives, in that they store and play back music stored in "zeros and ones" in its memory.
- **Blank Media-** While this is not a controlled item *per se*, a computer with a CD-RW drive left alone for a few minutes without its access locked risks an opportunistic attacker copying critical files.

The real question management must answer is how strict does the prohibition of controlled items need to be? Is it required for the facility as a whole, or should all items be allowed in unless they are expressly prohibited for a particular meeting? Are there particular areas of the facility with separate security procedures for which more stringent controls will be put in place? When visitors are going to be in the more-controlled facility, do they know beforehand that they will not be allowed to take certain controlled items into the meeting?

9.5.3   A Visitor's Physical and Network Access

In order to properly administer the policies described in this chapter, the organization must determine first where a visitor will be allowed to go without and escort and where they will only be allowed to go with an escort. All employees should know where visitors are allowed to go unattended and should be instructed to politely inquire when someone they don't know is in a part of the facility unescorted visitors are not normally allowed. Especially in smaller facilities, visitors will be given verbal permission to do such things as get a cup of coffee or go to the restroom by their host when their meeting is being held in the restricted part of the office. In addition, important clients are often allowed to roam freely without escort. It is important for an employee to know who these people are, but it is more important for an employee to ensure the person in the kitchen or walking the halls belongs there.

> **Important: Where are the places visitors get coffee, and where are the bathrooms?   Care should be taken to ensure visitors have access to both amenities with no escort required if possible.**

In handling a visitor's network access, several decisions must be made:

Will Access Be Granted in Any Form?
Many facilities require a user to be an employee assigned to the facility with no exceptions for visitors. While this does enhance security, it may cause people to be reluctant to come to the facility because of the lack of access. Significant numbers of mobile phones are now also email-capable with a cell phone connection, so this problem might not be as significant as it once was, but a balance between connectivity and security should be considered where possible.

What Form Will the Access Take and What Privileges Will Be Allowed?
Most visitor access will take the form of a guest login with restricted privileges, such as only access to the World Wide Web. Another consideration would be whether the access will be wireless or Ethernet-only. Wireless connectivity gives the flexibility of allowing the visitor to work anywhere in the facility, while restricting access to Ethernet allows security to know that if a visitor is accessing the network that they will be in a or in one of a limited number of locations.

Are Conference Rooms to Which Visitors are Sent to Wait Unattended Behind the Firewall?

In his book *The Art of Deception*; Mitnick and Simon (2002) describe an attack that took place at the office where an intruder pretended to be a person with a legitimate appointment and talked an eager-to-help front desk person into granting him access to a conference room while waiting for the appointment, which never materialized, to occur. While in the conference room, the intruder was able to gain access to critical data and get away with it without getting caught. By the time the ruse was discovered, it was far too late to do anything about it. How to recognize and defend against this and other such attacks are found in the discussion on social engineering.

9.6   Applying the Balanced Scorecard to Physical Security

The goals and their measures in establishing a reference Physical Security balanced scorecard are:

Goal: Ensure the networking hardware is in the best possible location.
- Server room configured appropriately-
  - o   Are the machines in good working order and verified as such regularly? How long ago did this last occur?
  - o   Are the necessary surge protectors and fire control equipment readily available and up-to-date? How long ago was this last verified?
  - o   Are all fire and other relevant safety codes being complied with and is this fact documented regularly? How long ago was this last verified?
- Risk from entrances not under direct organizational control is mitigated to the greatest extent possible
  - o   Is an access card for IT hardware areas only issued to only those employees with a bona fide reason to have access to the network equipment? When was the last inventory taken to validate this?
  - o   Are all means of accessing the facility and the server room alarmed to immediately notify a contract security company and/or law enforcement in place? When was this last verified?
  - o   Are the alarms tested on a regular basis? When was the last test performed?

- Procedure with current company and security company/law enforcement contact information is in place to deal with physical security incidents
    - o Is there a primary point of contact in the organization that will be notified immediately if an incident occurs? When was their contact information last verified?
    - o If an incident occurs during the middle of the night, will the method of contacting the organizational point of contact awaken them? How long ago was this last tested?
    - o If there is no response from the primary point of contact, is a secondary point of contact identified? How long ago was this last tested?
    - o When either or both points of contact are on travel or are otherwise unavailable, have alternates been identified and put in the incident response chain of communication? When were the points of contact last updated and the ability to reach them verified?
- Server room environment is controllable
    - o Is the climate control for the server room independent of all other controls? When was this last verified?
    - o Is there an alert system should the temperature in the server room rise above a certain level? How long ago was this last tested?

Goal: Ensure employees are readily identifiable
- Badges must be worn at all times
    - o Are employees always wearing their badges above the waste and with all relevant data visible? How often are visual inspections conducted?
    - o Are violations of the badge policy noted and corrective action taken? What percentage of badge policy violations have been dealt with according to policy?
- Badges should be designed to communicate all relevant information
    - o Do employee badges convey up-to-date information about the employee's status and privileges? How long ago was the information last verified?
    - o Do employee badge design elements have a uniform meaning across the organization? How long ago was the design validated as valid?

Goal: Ensure employee outprocessing is handled securely
- Collect all badges and access cards/keys

- o Is the organization aware of all badges issued to the employee? How long ago was the last badge audit conducted?
- o Is there a form signed by the employee acknowledging receipt of the badges and access cards or keys when issued and signed by an organization official when returned? What percentage of the badges, keys and access cards issued to employees have been signed for?
- o If a badge, access card or key is lost, is there a procedure to deactivate and badges and access card and to determine if it is necessary to change the locks to the doors the lost key opens? After a badge, access card or key is reported stolen, how long does it take to deactivate them or to change the locks if necessary?
- Collect organization-provided equipment
  - o Did the organization document all equipment issued to the employee? How long ago was this list last audited for accuracy?
  - o Did the employee sign a form acknowledging receipt of all equipment provided and will an organizational representative sign a form acknowledging the return of all organization-provided equipment? How long ago was this list last audited for accuracy?
- Restrict and/or monitor activity until transition is completed
  - o Is the outgoing employee to have their access restricted in any way until they have worked their last day? From the time the employee submits their resignation, how long does it take to restrict their privileges?
  - o Is the IT department to audit the outgoing employee's activities on the organization's network? During random inspections, how often has an outgoing employee requiring an escort been found unescorted?
  - o Is there a procedure in place to deal with a scenario in which the outgoing employee engages in suspicious behavior on the network? When an employee is found to be behaving suspiciously, how long does it take to remove the risk of their causing damage to the organization?
- Conduct exit interview
  - o Is a set exit interview procedure in place? What percentage of outgoing employees participate in the exit interview?

- o Is it an organizational policy to not speak ill of outgoing and former employees? How many times has this policy been violated?
- o Are outgoing employees encouraged to be forthright about their true reasons for leaving? How many comments from outgoing employees have proved to be useful to the organization?

Goal: Ensure visitor access is adequately controlled

- Are all means of entry to the facility monitored?
  - o Are all doors locked or alarmed unless a key or access card is used from the outside or an employee disarms the door? How often is this verified, and how many violations of this policy have occurred?
  - o Is a staffed reception desk located at all major entrance points to the facility? How many times has the desk been found to not be staffed for an unacceptable period of time?
- Are all visitors required to produce government-issued identification and to sign in?
  - o Is the reception staff trained to permit only those visitors who produce government-issued IDs or on the word of an employee? How many times has this policy been violated?
  - o Does the sign-in sheet capture all relevant information? When was the sign-in sheet last updated/validated?
- Are controlled items documented or collected as required?
  - o Is the reception staff trained on which items are not allowed to be brought into the facility? How long ago was the last training session?
  - o Is there a means of storing any collected items? When was the system last tested?
  - o Is there a policy (ejection, confiscation) to deal with prohibited items found on the premises? How many incidents have occurred?
- If an escort is required, is the policy enforced?
  - o Are visitor badges for those requiring escorts clearly marked? When was the badge design last validated?
  - o Are visitors requiring escorts found to be unescorted handled in accordance with an established policy? How many instances of unescorted guests have occurred?

o   Is there a policy in place to deal with an employee whose
visitor is found unescorted? How many instances of unescorted visitors have been documented?

9.7   Conclusion

Physical is the least glamorous of the security roles discussed in this
book, but it is at least as important, if not more so, then the use of technology to thwart attackers. Should an unauthorized person gain access to the
server room or even an Ethernet port behind an organization's firewall,
they could very well be able to browse your networks at will. Maintaining
careful control as to server room configuration, employee outprocessing
and employee and visitor badging is of critical importance in establishing a
facility's physical security.

9.8   Discussion Questions

Where is IT equipment for the office in which you work? Is anyone
able to walk in without needing a special key or keycard/badge? Who is
able to see the door to the room? How many people have a legitimate need
to get into the server room?

When was the last time someone checked to see if
*   All the equipment that is supposed to be in the server room is
    indeed there, and
*   There is no extra equipment, such as an extra backup or an un-
    authorized wireless access point?

How many people from your organization are in the facility daily? Do
you know all of them? Is seeing someone you don't know in your work
area a normal occurrence?

Do you have a way of distinguishing an employee with access to restricted areas from one who does not? If, for example, an employee badge
communicates this information, is there a policy in place that the badge not
be worn outside the organization?

When an employee resigns or is terminated, how are they handled? Is
there a set process to collect badges, keys and equipment? What would
your organization do if an employee resigned via email?

How does your organization handle visitors entering the facility? Are restricted areas clearly labeled? Is there a policy in place describing the actions to be taken in case a visitor is found in a restricted area?

Chapter 10 Disaster Recovery

Chapter Objectives

This chapter will discuss:
- Disaster Recovery is always a late-night phone call away,
- Factors to consider when formulating a Disaster Recovery Plan,
- An organization's business processes as the baseline for a disaster recovery strategy,
- Data's role in conceptualizing disaster recovery, and
- Steps to take in returning the damaged site to normal operations.

10.1 Disaster is Always Just around the Corner

In keeping with Murphy's Law, that whatever can go wrong will go wrong, and at the worst possible time, imagine you're sound asleep the night before the most important day of the organization's week, month, quarter or year. You went to bed a little early in order to be fresh and alert for the long day ahead. But while the day will be stressful, you know that everything is in place.

Suddenly, your peaceful slumber is interrupted by your home phone, cell phone and mobile email device all activating simultaneously. It turns out that the fire alarm system in your building has malfunctioned and deployed the sprinkler system. Water, a threat just as deadly to IT equipment as a human intruder, has destroyed at least some of your infrastructure. Because the deadlines you face cannot be pushed back, you are now forced to spring into action and activate the Disaster Recovery Plan, of which a critical part is the Business Continuity Plan.

Does your organization have a Disaster Recovery Plan? If you don't know if you have a plan, are you in a position of enough seniority that you should know? Rutberg (2005) shares the anecdote of a financial firm who fell victim to a disaster, and noted that the company had recently tested their plan and that it worked almost perfectly, with the exception of the phone list, which listed some people who were no longer with the company. The four or five critical people were constantly in contact with each other and by the next morning they had approximately one quarter of their staff of fifty-five working at their alternate work site and had not lost access to any of their customers or their data.

10.2 Factors to Be Considered in Formulating a Disaster Recovery Plan

There are several obvious potentialities that must be taken into account when determining how operations would continue in the event of a disruption, but others that may constitute a "disaster" for the organization that would not seem to be so normally. Terrari (2004) wrote that devising a plan consists of asking questions of oneself as to what would be required to keep the organization operating as normal as quickly as possible.

10.2.1 Acts of Nature

Is the organization located in an area that is prone to having major weather events? The staggering impact of Hurricane Katrina on New Orleans, even given the fact that the storm did not hit the city with the force expected, gives all the indication needed to recognize that almost everyone is vulnerable. Earthquakes and floods are two other possibilities. In addition, fires could utterly destroy an organization's physical infrastructure. No place is totally safe from natural disasters, so be certain to account for them in your risk calculations. Does the organization have adequate insurance to recover the damages suffered through an act of nature?

10.2.2 Human Acts

Much more common is a disruption caused by a person's or persons' actions. How much damage could a disgruntled employee accomplish if they were determined to hurt the organization as much as they could? If the IT equipment from your location was stolen, could the organization continue to function effectively? What if you are behind on the rent for your facility and are locked out of it by your landlord? The most famous recent human acts to disrupt operations were those on September 11, 2001, but nothing nearly as dramatic need occur to impact an individual organization.

> **Important:** Is your organization, as the joke says, "bus sensitive"?
> This means that if a particular person were to be hit by a bus on the
> way home tonight that your organization would lose a significant
> amount of its ability to function. Avoid this at all costs!

10.2.3 Distribution of Organizational Functionality among Various Locations

As will be discussed in the next section and in the final chapter, there is
a real need to understand the business processes an organization executes
in accomplishing its mission. In many cases, the business of an organization does not take place in a single location, but rather in many diverse locations, as seen in Chapter 2. Jackson (2000) refers to the distribution of
business processes across multiple physical locations as *functional interdependence.* After all, if the organization doesn't understand how it oper-
ates, it can't expect to be able to anticipate and defend against the potential
impacts of a disaster. In addition,

> "(c)ircumstances affecting   interdependencies revolve
> around rapid rates of change that most modern organiza-
> tions are going through.   These include reorganiza-
> tion/restructuring, personnel relocation, changes in the
> competitive environment, and outsourcing. Every time an
> organizational structure changes, the (Business Continuity
> Plan) had to change, and the interdependencies had to be
> reassessed. The more rapid the change, the more daunting
> the BCP reshuffling." (ibid)

> **Important:** In the interest of full disclosure, the author's full-time
> employment is with a company specializing in helping organizations
> identify their business processes and optimize how they leverage
> people, organizational structure and technology in conducting their
> business.

10.3 An Organization's Processes

It should go without saying that in order to construct a Disaster Recovery Plan or a Business Continuity Plan an organization must have a com-

prehensive grasp of the processes it implements as it goes about its daily business. The best way to do this is through an Enterprise Architecture, discussed in Chapter 18. For the specific purpose of a Disaster Recovery/Business Continuity Plan, processes may be divided into three categories: critical, preferable and optional.

Critical processes are those without which the organization would not be able to fulfill its obligations to customers, employees and constituents (shareholders, owners, other government entities, for example). If competitive advantage is created by field sales representatives enjoying instant access to inventory levels and quotes, mobile connectivity and availability of that information would be a critical process. Another example is the ability to implement what in the military is known as "focused logistics." In focused logistics, all or part of a delivery originally destined for one location is diverted to another, even while en route to the original destination. It could even be that a truck could be sent to an alternate location, such as a distribution center, to have the redirected portion of the load transferred to another vehicle. In this type of highly dynamic and tightly coupled environment several elements must come together to make it work:

- The need must be defined- In this case, a shortage must be identified and communicated to a system or person for purposes of fixing the problem.
- The immediate solution must be identified- Potential sources (trucks on the road, stock at a nearby warehouse, for example) must be known.
- The solution must be implemented- Truck drivers must be instructed to alter course, warehouse employees must be told how to adjust their loads, and the impacted locations must know the updated quantities to be received.
- The diverted materiel must be "backfilled"- While a higher priority arose, causing items to be diverted, the original requirement did not disappear. The system must now update to ensure the location originally intended to receive the goods gets them when possible.
- The system must be updated- When diversions occur, the system must be reset to reflect the optimal distribution solution possible given the new locations of goods and trucks. A useful analogy is when an airplane scheduled to fly is grounded for repair. Because of the tightly coupled nature of an airline's

schedule, sometimes planes are kept in reserve to enter the network when needed. If a plane is not available, the "hub and spoke" model of the airline industry is disrupted. If, for example, the grounded plane is a connecting flight upon which the itineraries of several travelers depend to make their flights to their final destination, and they miss their connections, then those passengers must be re-booked. This "cascade effect" is a major problem for airlines, as demonstrated in that it often takes two or three days for the system to return to normal operations. Until then, a constant reconfiguring of planes, flight crews and passengers creates quite a bit of confusion.

If any part of the IT environment required to perform the required functions did not function properly chaos would ensue.

Preferable functions are those that when not operational it is difficult and inefficient to implement the organization's business processes but not impossible. In this case, payroll processing is a good example.

Many, if not all, accountants have processed payroll manually at some point in their career, even if it was only to forward to a company hired to provide payroll processing services. If, for instance, a major system failure caused the service company to become unable to process its payroll, then an alternative must be found. Perhaps another service company could be found, but if not the process would need to be handled in-house. Because the payroll process would no longer be a routine function, time normally allotted for other duties would need to be dedicated to making sure everyone receives their paycheck or direct deposit on time, as failing to do so would be unacceptable.

Another example is the automatic aggregated reporting to managers of statistics used to measure how well the organization is functioning. In this case it should be emphasized that it is not the reporting itself that isn't critical but rather the automated nature of it that can be done without for a short time while operations are restored. As the systems serving as the "authoritative source" for the data used to compose the report are brought back online the data can be put into an Excel spreadsheet for the manager's consumption until the reporting functionality is working again. Should real-time decisions need to be made, such as in the logistics example above, the situation qualifies for "critical" status, but if the reports are done weekly, monthly or quarterly then they can wait while truly critical functionality is restored. Good luck explaining to the manager that their report isn't "critical to the business continuity of the organization."

Optional functions are those people "like to have" but are not necessary to implement an organization's business processes. In fact, when an optional functionality is lost it may be evaluated to see if it's missed since it went away. If not, then perhaps it could be turned off permanently.

Has the plan to restore business operations been tested? While many ideas work in theory, the way to be most confident a plan will succeed is to hold periodic training exercises in which a scenario is played out as realistically as possible. This is an inconvenience for the staff to go through, but it is necessary. To reinforce the priority it has, senior leaders should also be involved. A good way to increase involvement and buy-in is to ask employees about incidents they've been involved with in the past and solicit their input as to what they thought went well and not so well in their employer's response. Not only are the employees empowered through their involvement, but they could very well help you come up with a better response or maybe even bring up a scenario that had yet to be planned out.

Figure 10.1 describes The Disaster Recovery/Business Continuity Plan.

Plans	Goals, objectives, schedules relative to disaster recovery
Processes	<ul><li>Methodology for handling disaster</li><li>Notification process</li><li>Process for having information vital to the recover of a disaster available</li><li>Process for maintaining/updating the plan, processes, procedures, roles, and responsibilities</li></ul>
People	<ul><li>Roles and responsibilities of the Disaster Recovery Coordinator</li><li>Roles and responsibilities of the Disaster Recovery Team</li></ul>
Procedures	<ul><li>Recovery procedures and procedure tests</li><li>Disaster simulations</li><li>Assessment simulations</li><li>Call-out lists (primary and backup)</li><li>Pointer/access to performance indices</li><li>Pointer/access to most recent equipage listing</li><li>Pointer/access to most recent data backup</li><li>Pointer/access to spare inventory</li></ul>

Figure 10.1 "The Four Ps": Plans, Processes, People and Procedures (adapted from Baker, et al, 2004)

The "Four Ps" from the figure: plans, processes, people and procedures, synthesize disaster recovery and business continuity into four easily remembered categories. Under the "people" column, it should be noted that two roles, Disaster Recovery Coordinator and Disaster Recovery Team, have been named. These positions should not be "one-deep," however; there should be people assigned as backups in case the primary point of contact is not available.

10.4 Data as a Critical Element of Business Continuity

The one common element across all of the examples discussed directly above is data. Without data, it is impossible to analyze what is being done or even to know what needs to be done in support of the organization. This will be discussed more fully in Chapter 18, but the basic questions to be answered are:

- *What data do we have?* As the organization goes about its business, data is generated. All data generated may be analyzed.
- *Which systems generate the data to be analyzed?* In order for data to be reliable for analysis, there should be a single "authoritative source" for each piece of data. In the U.S. government, laws, regulations and policies sometimes force data to be found in multiple areas. Because it does not always come from the same source, there are data quality problems in parts of the DOD. Even in cases where data is simply copied from one system into another, bandwidth issues arise as well as transmission errors. In certain parts of the DOD, millions of transactions occur each month. If even a few percent of the records are lost when crossing the interface, an accurate picture of the current situation will be lost. In the case of financial records, the ability to perform a "clean" audit would not exist. To close the books, rework to find lost records and put them in the system of record must be undertaken, wasting time and resources.
- *What are our legal obligations with the data?* As discussed in Chapter 8, laws such as Sarbanes-Oxley obligate organizations to provide not only financially accurate data but also protect the personal health information of those people whose information the organization controls. As the examples of Chapter 1 illustrate, there are myriad ways for information to be lost or obtained surreptitiously.

- *Do we have backup copies and emergency systems?* A key consideration is the ability to move as seamlessly as possible to a backup system. For critical functions, the move should be transparent. Another decision to be made is how often to backup the data, how many copies are to be made and where they are to be stored. If the main systems are rendered inoperable, is another on standing by to take over?
- *How will customers and other members of the extended enterprise be able to access the data they need?* Even if an organization's office building burns down to the ground, that doesn't mean those relying on its data are able to wait for everything to be rebuilt. While spare email servers are easy to stand up and backup data can be input into the backup systems, it is equally critical that those external to the organization are able to get to their data.

Without the correct data flowing as needed across business processes, an organization will not be able to function as it should. The focus of any and all disaster recovery operations should be to restore data flow as quickly and completely as possible. The way to do this is to ensure the proper people, systems and functions communicate as they should.

10.5 Restoring the Original Site

While the work to continue the organization's business is going on, the process to restore the damaged facility to its prior condition must begin. Dorf and Johnson (2000) discuss the process for doing so. The first priority, of course, is to ensure that no-one is endangered physically by the situation. Unsafe areas should be marked off and access should be prohibited. If alarms were activated and have not yet been reactivated they should be turned back on as quickly as possible without their interfering with the restoration work. If it is impossible to turn the systems back on it may be best to assign a security officer to guard the facility to deter anyone who might be tempted to enter the facility without authorization.

First, establish a log documenting all steps taken by the organization in handling the restoration.

To mitigate the risk of complicating the insurance process, the organization's insurance company and the property management company (if the facility is leased) should be notified immediately. To protect against the elements, any damaged parts of the facility should be covered as completely as possible. After inspecting the damage, arrange for any required environmental (heat and water removal, for example) services to be provided. Once the area has been deemed safe to enter, photograph the scene to provide documentation for insurance purposes. Recover all equipment, hard copy documents and media for inspection and data repair/data recovery. If the damage is extensive and interrupts business consider bringing in an accountant expert in the field to assist in determining the extent of the damages to be claimed.

After documenting the damage, submit the materials to the insurance adjuster and work with the adjuster in their inspection of the facility. Receive permission to proceed with repairs and purchase of major items. Negotiate the final claim amount and "submit a sworn proof of loss to the insurance company." (ibid)

10.5 Applying the Balanced Scorecard to Disaster Recovery

The goals and their measures in establishing a reference Disaster Recovery balanced scorecard are:

Goal: Know a disaster is occurring as quickly as possible.
- Alert process arranged properly-
    - o Who is the point of contact to be reached by the security company or the authorities in case of an emergency? How long ago was the contact information last updated?
    - o If the point of contact is not available, who gets called next? How long ago was the contact information last updated?
    - o Does each employee have, at home, a list of people to call to notify an emergency has happened? How long ago was the list last updated?
- Duties are assigned-
    - o Have the actions to be taken in case of foreseeable scenarios been identified and allocated? How long ago was this plan last updated?
    - o Are all those assigned duties in case of an emergency still with the organization? How long ago was this list last updated?

o Are alternate points of contact identified? How long
   ago was this list last updated?
o Do the responsible parties have, in hard copy, the procedures they are to follow in case of an emergency?
   (Remember, emergencies tend to happen in the middle
   of the night.) How long ago were the procedures last
   updated?

Goal: Identify potential disaster scenarios
- Generic disaster scenarios identified-
  - o On what floor or floors are your facilities? How long
       ago was the list last updated?
  - o Has there ever been an emergency there before? How
       well did the property managers and insurance compa-
       nies handle it? Based on various performance catego-
       ries, how well did they handle the emergency?
- Area-specific disaster scenarios identified-
  - o Is your facility in a flood-prone zone or in an area in
       which earthquakes are common? How long ago was the
       disaster potential of your organization's facilities up-
       dated?

Goal: Identify organizational functional interdependence
- Impact of emergency assessed-
  - o What business processes does your facility execute?
       How long ago was this updated?
  - o If your facility were to go offline completely, what
       would be the impact to you? How long ago was the
       business continuity plan last updated?
  - o If your facility were to go offline completely, what
       would be the impact to the organization as a whole?
       How long ago were damage scenario assessments last
       performed?
  - o For any single or combination of systems or processes
       disabled by an emergency, what would be the impact on
       your facility and the organization as a whole? How
       long ago was this assessment last performed?
- Recourse in case of facility disablement documented-

o   Is an alternate work facility available? What percentage of the main site could be accommodated by the alternate site or sites?

o   Is it possible for the entire workforce to telecommute if necessary? What percentage of the workforce could telecommute?

Goal: Restore functionality as a function of process priority

- Backup strategy validated-
    o   Where are the facility's backups located? How long ago was the facility last inspected?
    o   Is the alternate facility able to handle information stored on your backup medium (such as magnetic tape)? How long ago was the backup infrastructure verified as to its good working order?
- Order of system restoration established-
    o   Have the facility's business processes been identified and prioritized? How long ago was this last updated?
    o   Has this prioritization been reflected in the order in which the facility's IT systems are restored? When was this list last updated?

Goal: Ensure data is handled as necessary

- Organizational data responsibilities established
    o   For which data in your organization is an IT system from your facility the authoritative source? How long ago was this last validated?
    o   How often is your data backed up?
    o   How will those within your extended enterprise be made able to access the data they need to see? How long ago was this system last tested?
- Legal data responsibilities established-
    o   Which data elements in IT systems your facility controls are subject to laws or regulations defining how they are to be handled? How long ago was this list last validated?
    o   Are the controls on the data automatically enabled when the alternate systems are turned on or is additional work required to enable them? How long ago was this last tested?

Goal: Restore the damaged site to its original condition

- Documentation process established-
  - o Does the organization have a documentation process pre-coordinated with the insurance company or companies? How long ago was the process last updated?
  - o Are all points of contact trained in following the proper documentation procedures? How long ago was the training last held?
- Physical safety established-
  - o Has the location been isolated and secured? How long does/did it take to secure the facility during a disaster?
  - o Have any parts of the facility exposed to the elements been covered as well as possible to prevent further damage? How long after it was safe to enter the facility was it protected from the elements?
- Finalize insurance settlement-
  - o Has the organization received permission to proceed with repairs and order major items? How long does/did it take the insurance company to authorize repairs?
  - o Has the final insurance claim been submitted in compliance with insurance company requirements? What was the accuracy of the initial insurance claim?

10.6 Conclusion

A disaster recovery strategy is an inconvenience until it is needed, at which point it is absolutely critical to execute the strategy correctly. Employee safety must be ensured, insurance companies must be notified, and procedures to re-establish business functionality must be followed. If the process is not followed correctly, business disruptions may be disrupted and insurance claims could be rejected.

10.7 Discussion Questions

If you were to receive a call tonight that your facility was being flooded or was on fire, what would you do? Whom would you call?

Think about your own job in terms of what you do on a daily basis. What data do you need to access? Where does it come from? If the IT system you or your point of contact wasn't available, how would you do your job?

Think about your job in terms of how it fits into your organization as a whole. Of which business line, if any, are you a part? In addition to those you depend on to do your job, who depends on the data or other outputs you provide to do their job?

Chapter 11 Initial Employee Communication

Chapter Objectives

This chapter will discuss:
- The overall purpose of communication in establishing an employee's work environment
- Five types of information an employee could handle in the course of their work
- The role of employee agreements in establishing an employee's responsibilities to the organization regarding proprietary information
- Employee rights and responsibilities regarding organization-issued equipment and equipment brought onto organization premises
- The organization's policies toward monitoring employee behavior regarding personal communication while working, and
- The consequences an employee could face in the case of unauthorized information release or other unapproved communication behavior

11.1 The Overall Purpose of Initial Employee Communication

When a new employee joins an organization, it is important to establish a realistic picture in their mind of their rights and responsibilities with regard to their new place of work. For information security the real issue comes in, for most organizations, the balance between providing good internal and external responsiveness and protecting the organization from internal and external threats. The potential consequences of a security breach are so high that every reasonable precaution should be taken to guard against losing confidential or individual data. Initial and ongoing employee communication and training should be seen as a means to help employees understand their role in security as well as potentially inoculate the organization in the case of a breach.

Another aspect of security when an employee joins an organization is the decision that must be made by the company as to where to strike the balance between ensuring its security and imposing too many restrictions on its employees. Workers are willing to tolerate only so many constraints in relation to their level of compensation. A very fine line exists between keeping otherwise lazy workers vigilant and forcing good employees out of the organization because the level of monitoring they face every day is more than they are willing to endure.

> **Important:** The author is not a lawyer and is therefore not able to render legal opinions or give legal advice. Terms used may not be the most appropriate ones when applied in a legal context and should be interpreted as coming from a layperson and intended for a layperson. All statements in this chapter and the book as a whole should be viewed as discussion points and concepts rather than legal advice, including those passages in which a licensed attorney is cited, as their publicly available works may contain a similar disclaimer. It is strongly recommended that you consult a licensed attorney in your jurisdiction should any question about relevant laws and precedents applying to your particular situation arise.

11.2 Some Examples of "Confidential Information"

An important question to ask and answer thoroughly is "What information, in isolation or in combination with other information, would compromise this organization?" In much simpler times, hard copies of documents and drawings kept in secure locations were the only records of an organization's confidential data, very few people had access to the areas in which the physical records were held and the only way to get the records out was to hand-copy them or smuggle in a camera to take a picture of the material. Now, of course, while access is limited and shredders have been deployed throughout many organizations, there are many more ways to access and make off with an organization's data. In answering this question, several types and sources of information must be brought into the equation.

Technical Information- As addressed in the discussion on social engineering elsewhere in the book, being able to gain access to a competitor's research and development, product, or other information will allow the party doing the stealing to much more easily develop a product and get it to market or to the patent office before your organization can. For many high-tech firms, foreign agents are now in the business of penetrating the organization. For another example of how commercial spying has replaced government-to-government spying, read about how Russia has repurposed some of its former KGB officers into industrial spies see Knight (1997).

Company Information- Would you think a company phone book, organizational chart and some web pages describing your products or services would be enough for a competitor to gain a good bit of knowledge about your plans? It would almost certainly be enough, and that's not the only information available. If you work for a private company and have received funding from an angel investor or a venture capitalist, knowledge of the product that won the investment would enable a potential competitor to know specifically what piqued their interest and would give the competitor a path forward they would not have otherwise had. At risk is that they devise a better product idea and the investor decides to fund "their" idea instead of yours.

"Regulated" Information- In this case, "regulated" information is information not allowed to be disclosed as a result of a government law or regulation. Specific examples of laws creating the need for regulations to be drafted by U.S. government executive agencies are the Health Insurance Portability and Accountability Act and Sarbanes-Oxley. These laws are discussed in detail elsewhere.

Contacts and Calendars- Wouldn't you like to know who your competitors have lunch with on a regular basis or meet with regularly? Do they act as if they have a strong connection with someone or a certain company or government official? A misplaced or stolen appointment book or cell phone/personal digital assistant could divulge all that information and more. While admittedly an extreme case, it could be that someone might be hired to steal a briefcase, laptop or personal communication device.

Classified Information- In the U.S., access to national security and law enforcement information is controlled by levels of classification such as "Secret", "Top Secret" and others. When this book was written, a major investigation into the leaking of classified information involving the release of the identity of a CIA operative with the Directorate of Operations (the clandestine service), who was undercover and the Agency was actively working to keep her identity unknown seemed to be coming to an end. In addition, a veteran CIA analyst had been fired for having unauthorized contact with a reporter. In neither case was the illegal transfer of classified information part of the publicly known allegations, but in one case the prosecutor investigated the possibility of bringing criminal charges against targets of his investigation and in the other it is thought that the unauthorized contact involved the transfer of classified information.

These five types of information and others that may apply to one's organization should be considered when crafting policies and procedures. With them in mind, mechanisms to help protect an organization will now be discussed.

11.3 Non-Disclosure Agreements

"To strengthen their positions in legal battles to protect trade secrets, employers should consider addition additional steps to enhance the secrecy and security of confidential information." (Dubberly, 1998) A key document to design and have each new employee sign before being given access to any company data is a non-disclosure agreement (NDA). The simple interpretation of an NDA is that the employee agrees to not reveal any information about the organization to those without the need to know it. Dubberly (ibid) highlights several key points to be addressed in an NDA.

First, the "legal playing field" should be specified in the agreement. Based on the advice of the organization's legal team, "the forum selection, choice of venue and law clauses" should be chosen to provide the organization with the legal environment most advantageous to its needs. Because different jurisdictions may have different laws and precedents, what may be deemed enforceable in one court may not be ruled identically in another court.

Second, "a provision permitting the employer to assign the agreement without the employee's consent to any successor, joint venture partner, or corporate parent, affiliate, or subsidiary of the employer" should be included. This will prevent an employee from leaving the organization in the case of a merger or acquisition and being able to claim that because the employer no longer exists that they are no longer bound by the NDA.

Third, "a clause requiring the employee to inform any subsequent employer about the agreement" should be added. This will serve to inform the new employer that any confidential information from their current organization is legally protected. It would seem from a non-legal perspective that there would be a significant area for literal and figurative judgments to be made to determine when communicating one's expertise moves from unprotected to protected knowledge. We may refer to patent law to elaborate on the subject. Stim and Pressman (2004) note that in the U.S., for example, published or otherwise publicly available information, known as "prior art" in patent terms, would cause a patent application to be rejected because it would be considered as having entered the public domain.

It is important to consider, therefore, where to draw the line between allowing potential clients to understand your unique offerings versus protecting the rights to enforce intellectual property law against those who would seek to take your methods for their own purposes. Some organizations, especially those founded by academics, place a large emphasis on publishing journal articles and books about their field. In making that choice, however, there is always a risk that something that may invalidate an intellectual property claim could be released to the public. If this is seen as a realistic possibility, a part of the NDA could be that any works composed about a work-relevant topic by an employee must first be reviewed by the organization before it may be published.

Fourth, a "tattle-tale provision requiring the employee to report to the employer all unauthorized disclosures or uses of the employer's trade secrets or confidential information that come to the employee's attention" should be part of any agreement (Dubberly, 1998) This can have a very strong deterrent effect, as it is difficult for one person to conceal disallowed behavior for an extended period of time. In addition, conspiracies among multiple parties often are broken up when one member of the group gets into trouble and then decides to provide information on their co-conspirators in exchange for leniency. As mentioned in the social engineering discussion, the very best scam artists are rarely caught or even noticed, however.

Finally, a "clause providing that if the employee has a question about whether specific information is considered confidential, he or she must request a written clarification from a designated [organization] official" should be included. This serves to provide more clarity into the responsibilities of an employee. There is now substantially less cause, it would seem, for an employee to be able to claim ignorance because no-one told them if the information they had was confidential or public.

11.4 Non-Compete Agreements

A second type of agreement to include when an employee joins an organization is a "non-compete agreement", in which the new hire promises to not compete against the organization for a specified period of time after they have left the organization. In general terms, it is important to establish in your organization's thinking as to what exactly it would mean for someone to "compete" against you and how you would need to go about protecting the organization from someone "crossing the street" and joining a rival. Two key issues to be addressed are the scope of activities you want to prohibit and the length of time for which competition will be prohibited.

In deciding the activities to be prohibited by the agreement, a major consideration is the enforceability of the agreement. While many would assume that an employee's signature on a document would mean that "that's the deal, and you're stuck with it," that does not seem to be the case. Gilman, for example, notes that "employee non-competition agreements are unenforceable in some states." (1990)

Another issue comes in determining the definition of what you mean. For example, if the agreement an organization's employees sign prohibits them from competing in the same "business line" or "industry" and the name of the line or industry is named, what are the legal implications of that wording? Only competent legal advice can answer these questions.

In addition to the activities prohibited by the agreement, the length of time a former employee will be prohibited from competing is also at issue. Is one year enough? Gilman (1990) suggests two or three years. From a layperson's business perspective, the organization would best be protected by a period of time after which the former employee's knowledge would have become out of date.

Important: In researching this chapter and in the author's non-legal but real-world experience, this area of the law in the U.S. is murky at best, so it is strongly recommended that an organization take great care in constructing its non-disclosure and non-compete agreements.

11.5 Policies Relative to Employee IT Use

In balancing between an organization's right and responsibility to protect its information from unauthorized dissemination and the willingness of an employee to tolerate "Big Brother" watching over their shoulder, decisions must be made as to how much oversight should be used. Some of this discussion is also addressed in the chapter on Physical Security from the standpoint of an organization's visitors.

11.5.1 Inspection of IT-Applicable Devices Brought Onto Organization Property

The title for this subsection is awkwardly worded in that "IT-applicable" may not seem to make sense at first reading. Isn't it obvious what a piece of information technology is? No-one would argue that a desktop or laptop computer is IT hardware, but is a cell phone? Is an iPod? The technically savvy readers will know that anything that can transfer files to and from a computer could serve as a "Sneaker Net" to remove information from an organization.

As discussed in the chapter on Physical Security, there could be a need to establish a policy forbidding IT-applicable devices from being brought into the part of an organization's facility in which sensitive information is available. In some government facilities, for example, mobile phones with cameras are prohibited. Anyone who has read spy novels from the 1960 through the 1980s will no doubt remember the heroes or villains using small cameras to take pictures of important documents and then shipping the film in tiny containers back to the home office for analysis. Now, a person can take a picture, save it and email it from the same device. Unless a flash is used, it may not even be obvious the person is taking a picture and sending emails from one's phone is very normal nowadays. The trade off, of course, is that some people will be angered by the perceived lack of trust shown in being forced to check in or turn off their devices. This feeling is understandable, but anyone who has worked in a department store requiring that their bags be searched when they leave work at night or that they carry a special purse made of clear plastic (think a large sandwich bag) would know that this is a common level of security.

11.5.2 Policies Governing IT Equipment Use

The extent to which an employee is allowed to alter the default configuration for a computer is a major consideration for an organization. It's well-known that applications downloaded from the internet may contain some type of malware or might cause a conflict in the system, rendering at least some of its functionality inoperative. One, albeit restrictive, solution is to mandate that all similar pieces of IT equipment (such as all desktop computers) be configured identically and denies the individual user the ability to change the configuration or to install additional applications on the machine. This setup, known as a "burned image", simplifies the IT department's job, but at the cost of denying individual users the ability to tailor their device to fit their own requirements. In a part of the organization in which the job is very well-defined a burned image works well, while in parts of the organization in which workers may need to perform different types of work based on their unique requirements of that day.

"Exception Management", when a user is allowed to install an application on their system in addition to the default configuration, is a key consideration. Downloading games off the internet would almost certainly not be allowed, but there should be an efficient process in place for an employee to gain permission to vary from the default setup. Policies may differ among parts of an organization based on the needs of the employee and the nature of the information the employee's device is able to access.

Another aspect of an individual's use of IT devices in conducting the organization's business is whether and how to monitor the employee's email and internet traffic while they are on the job or using organization-provided equipment during non-work hours. There has been significant discussion on this topic in the U.S. as to what extent an employer may monitor an employee's activities while on the job, but it seems that in general the conclusion is that the employer does indeed have that right.

One area of interest is in the monitoring of emails and internet surfing while on the job. As seen in discussions elsewhere in the book, the information communicated to others within the organization and especially to those outside of the organization could give away the information the organization uses to keep itself ahead of the competition. Real-time monitoring is difficult, but searching archived emails periodically is recommended. In fact, a relevant question is "Does this position require the employee to have access to email from this workstation?" Would it be better to provide a separate workstation from which an employee is able to access email? Is it best to disable all drives (floppy, CD Read/Write and USB) that would allow someone to copy data from the computer and walk away with it?

For internet surfing, if it is allowed, is it monitored? Does the organization have a policy, such as "at no time shall an employee use (this organization's) equipment or networks to access pornography"? Should non-work related surfing be allowed? Some organizations block access to such sites as Yahoo! and Hotmail, while others also block CNN, ESPN and other similar sites. Be certain to balance what constitutes reasonable restrictions, as many people who work in these information-intensive positions will often be young enough that they have always been accustomed to having at least some access to their friends during the day. To shut them off from the "outside world" for the entire workday could be something they are not willing to abide for very long. As anyone who knows the way organizations function, the first problem is hiring the right people for the position, and the second is keeping them on the job. A constant need to replace employees in any position, much less one in which they have access to confidential information, is expensive and time consuming.

11.6 The Consequences of Violating the Employee Agreement

While it is unpleasant to do so, it is vital that an organization explain to its employees not only what is expected of them in security but what the possible consequences may be if they violate the policies and/or a law while with the organization. Perhaps the worker may not understand when they first join the organization that they personally could be responsible personally for the consequences of a security breach. The organization could be at risk as well, of course. A technique organizations use to empower its employees with the ability to detect and thwart an attempt to penetrate the organization is security training, which is discussed in another chapter. The argument, as told to the author during several training sessions he has attended at various organizations, is to help an employee know how to do their job as best they can with regard to security. If the employee has been trained, the explanation they give in the case of an incident is critical.

Ultimately, the company and enforcement officials must decide whether the incident was preventable, and if it was the extent to which the employee acted to prevent it versus the expected level of effort. Should an employee understand their job and establish that they acted reasonably; the consequences would not be nearly as severe as they would be if the employee is found to have cut corners or been irresponsible in another way. If it is found that the employee did act improperly, the organization is then evaluated to see if they had adequately trained the employee in how they were *supposed* to have behaved during the incident. If it can be shown that appropriate training was given, the organization will have a better chance of having its punishment lessened or even eliminated. What this means, of course, is that the employee is now forced to respond to any allegations personally, rather than through the organization. This could lead to great personal expense and involve significant personal risk, so it is very important that employees understand the possible consequences of negligence before they begin their new position. It would be very bad for an organization to earn a reputation for having its employees have legal trouble often. It may be assumed that many workers will not have the financial resources to defend themselves with an elite legal team, so care should be taken to ensure training is complete and understandable. While prevention is the first concern, should an incident occur some options to be considered to decrease the risk of future incidents are now discussed.

First, the employee could be made aware of the incident and should be required to cooperate fully with any resulting investigation. It is highly recommended that this condition be part of all employee agreements if legally permissible. Not only will the employee be aware of the incident and often able to aid the organization in reconstructing how it happened, but it will also help in preparing real-world case studies for future training sessions. Should the violation be determined to be of lesser severity, the employee could receive counseling and retraining on the relevant topic. If the issue is not yet covered in training, the employee could be given the opportunity to help the organization in formulating a training module on the topic, which would simultaneously retrain them on the issue and give them the ability to commit a positive act on behalf of the organization.

Should it be found that the employee did not show proper diligence but was neither severely negligent nor corrupt in their actions retraining and some form of formal documentation (being "written up" is the American slang term for this) may be made in addition to any necessary counseling and re-training. Should incidents of this severity occur multiple times more severe sanctions may then be considered.

If the employee is found to have acted with significant negligence, to the point of potentially exposing the company to, for example, legal jeopardy, penalties including transfer out of their current position of trust and into what should be a less well-paying job in a non-sensitive area of the company may be necessary. Other measures such as suspension, official warning and termination may also be necessary. Finally, there should be well-defined "firing offenses", in which case an employee will be terminated immediately should they be discovered to have committed certain acts of gross negligence or engaged in potentially criminal behavior. Management should determine the steps to be taken in the event of an incident of this magnitude. Will the employee be escorted from the building immediately, or should they be required to stay and answer questions? Will they have been required to consent to having their personal belongings, including all IT-relevant devices, searched?

Important: In determining the measures to be taken in the case of an incident it is of paramount importance that management understand the organization's rights within its legal jurisdiction. What may be allowed at one location may not be so at another. The rights of an organization to protect itself could be an important consideration when deciding the location of an office.

11.7 Applying the Balanced Scorecard to Initial Employee Communication

Some goals and their measures in establishing a reference Initial Employee Communication balanced scorecard are:

Goal: Define the Proper Legal Environment
- Identify Information to be Protected-
    - o What information does the organization create or consume that is of business value? How long ago was this list last updated?
    - o What information does the organization create or consume that is protected by laws or regulations? How long ago was this list last updated?
    - o Does the legal jurisdiction in which the organization currently operates meet the needs of the organization in protecting itself? How long ago was the governing legal jurisdiction evaluated for suitability?

Goal: Create the Proper Legal Documents

- Create Documents to Communicate Employee Responsibilities in Protecting Confidential Information
    - o Has an Employee Agreement been composed and reviewed by the business and legal authorities for completeness and correctness? When was the last review performed?
    - o Does the Employee Agreement contain language that protects the organization from an employee disclosing confidential information? When was the language last reviewed for currency?
    - o Does the Employee Agreement contain language that protects the organization from an employee from joining a competing organization for an adequate period of time? When was the language last reviewed for currency?
    - o Does the Employee Agreement adequately address the fact that an employee found to have acted negligently or illegally could be required to answer legal charges as an individual? When was the language last reviewed for currency?
    - o Should an employee transferring into a position in which confidential data is used be required to sign a different employee agreement as a condition for assuming the position? What percentage of employees have been allowed to assume new duties before signing a new employee agreement?

Goal: Ensure the Organization is Able to Inspect IT-Relevant Devices as Required and Allowed by Law

- Does the Employee Agreement address the organization's and the employee's rights and responsibilities for IT devices?
    - o Is the Employee Agreement legally enforceable? How was the employee agreement last reviewed?
    - o Does the Employee Agreement include or establish the proper legal setting for the organization's IT device inspection policies? How long ago was this verified?
    - o Does the Employee Agreement include or establish the proper legal setting for controlling an employee's ability to access personal email and non-work internet sites? How long ago was this last verified?
    - o Does the Employee Agreement include or establish the proper legal setting for monitoring an employee's

online activities while at work? How long ago was this verified?

11.8 Conclusion

Establishing a realistic picture in an employee's mind when they first join an organization or when they transfer into a new part of the organization as to their conduct and their rights and the rights of the organization with regard to communicating confidential information is vital to in many ways. From the positive perspective, an employee who wants to perform their duties to the best of their ability on behalf of the organization should be well-informed as to what is acceptable and what is unacceptable in the ways in which they dispense information. From the negative point of view, it is also important that an employee understand the importance of following established procedures and of the range of possible consequences should they violate any part of their employee agreement and/or organization information security procedures.

11.9 Discussion Questions

In your organization, what information exists that should be controlled?
- Human Resources data?
- Proprietary information, including technical and financial information and contact information?
- Classified information?
- Unclassified information that is governed by laws or regulations?

Does your organization require a new hire to sign an Employee Agreement?
- If not, are there plans to begin doing so?
- Have you been informed by legal counsel of the rights of and responsibilities incumbent upon the employee and organization in your jurisdiction?
- Have you determined the appropriate role of an Employee Agreement for your organization?
  o Prevent competition?
  o Prevent the release of certain information?
  o Mitigate legal consequences to the organization in the event of a security incident?
  o Allow for verifying policies are being followed?

- Monitoring email?
- Monitoring internet surfing?
- Monitoring phone calls?

Chapter 12 The Human Element

Chapter Objectives

This chapter will discuss:
- The role of the human being in an organization's security,
- The concept of the "mosaic" technique of intelligence gathering,
- The idea of a "social engineer" and how they operate,
- Some ways a social engineer may be defended against, and
- How an organization can integrate the human element into its balanced scorecard.

12.1 Humans- The Weakest Link in the Chain

Con men, rip-off artists, scammers, snake oil salesmen, whatever you call them, there are people in our world whose chosen profession is to trick us into revealing information to them that they have no legitimate right to know for use to their advantage. As noted in the chapter on Physical Security, the first line of defense may be a locked door or, appropriate to the technical discussion earlier in the book, a log-in screen, but none of that matters if someone is able to bypass the defenses. In some cases, being able to gain the needed access is shockingly easy, as will be discussed later in the chapter. The type of theft may be thought of in two different ways. First, *direct theft* is when an intruder gains unauthorized access and is able to get away with a program, formula or marketing plan, for example that gives the information's recipient an advantage they otherwise would not have enjoyed. With such information, a competitor would be able to beat the developer to market or would be able to reverse-engineer the design or code in order to build their own "copycat" product with most of the research and development done for the cost of stealing the information.

The second type of theft may be referred to as *indirect theft*. This type of theft occurs when an individual or group of individuals accumulate sufficient information to be able to discern a competitor's confidential data or strategies without (sometimes, arguably) needing to commit an actual crime. In fact, indirect methods may be used to enable a perpetrator to commit a direct act against an organization, as will be discussed in a moment when social engineering is addressed. The technique, known as constructing a "mosaic", is a powerful tool in intelligence gathering and analysis.

12.1.1 The Intelligence "Mosaic"

The American Heritage Dictionary (2004) defines "mosaic" as:

"1. (a) A picture or decorative design made by setting small colored pieces, as of stone or tile, into a surface. (b) The process or art of making such pictures or designs.
"2. A composite picture made of overlapping, usually aerial, photographs.
"3. Something that resembles a mosaic: *a mosaic of testimony from various witnesses.*"

As the definition moves from its most common usage (1) to least common (3), it becomes more relevant to the discussion at hand. The method describes a composite of information gathered and combined to reach a conclusion, based on independent inputs for analysis. A key technique in crime scene investigation is to ensure eyewitnesses talk with each other as little as possible, as their memories may be influenced through talking with other witnesses. While it may be more convenient to collect consistent input from all sources, there is a chance the collective memory will be incorrect. Rather, as social scientists have learned through training and other intellectually capable readers not having experienced the joy that is a formal social science education will remember from the popular and well-researched book *The Wisdom of Crowds* (Surowiecki, 2004), it is critical to gather as many credible and *independent* inputs as possible when evaluating a situation in dispute the adjudicator did not witness personally.

The field most commonly associated with the mosaic approach is espionage. The U.S. Congress' Joint Inquiry into the September, 2001 terrorist attacks noted that:

> "Intelligence analysts tend to reach conclusions based upon disparate fragments of data derived from widely-distributed sources and assembled into a probabilistic 'mosaic' of information. They seek to distinguish 'signals' from a bewildering universe of background 'noise' and make determina-

tions upon the basis of vague pattern recognition, inferences (including negative inferences), context, and history. For them, information exists to be *cross-correlated*—evaluated, and continually subjected to re-evaluation, in light of the total context of what is available to the organization as a whole. Intelligence analysts think in degrees of possibility and probability, as opposed to categories of admissibility and degrees of contribution to the ultimate criminal-investigative aim of proof 'beyond a reasonable doubt.'" (Joint Inquiry Into Intelligence Community Activities, 2002 [italics in original])

In the post-9/11 world, we have now become familiar with the U.S. National Security Agency's collecting international communications of American citizens in addition to those of foreign nationals in the U.S. as well as communications entirely outside its borders. Before this signals intelligence (SIGINT) was in the fore of the intelligence debate the role of human intelligence gathering was of concern in the U.S., at least in the realm of those concerned with technology transfer. The congressional report popularly known as *The Cox Report* (*House Report 105-851,* 1999) discussed the role of Chinese nationals in the U.S. collecting technical information for use to the benefit of Chinese interests.

"The PRC's twenty-year intelligence collection effort against the U.S. has been aimed at (capturing U.S. nuclear technology information). The PRC employs a 'mosaic' approach that capitalizes on the collection of small bits of information by a large number of individuals, which is then pieced together in the PRC. This information is obtained through espionage, rigorous review of U.S. unclassified technical and academic publications, and extensive interaction with U.S. scientists and Department of Energy laboratories." (*House Report 105-851,* 1999)

Because western democracies are very willing to permit scientific exchange rather than defining almost everything as classified, countries wishing to develop technologically must only read western technical literature and attend western universities to help their country gain valuable information in improving their technological abilities. The larger question of whether the benefits of free and open scientific dialog outweigh the gains enjoyed by competitor nations is a good one, but not relevant to our discussion. Instead, the mosaic as a method will be described in examples.

12.1.2 Building a Sample Mosaic

An Open Source Mosaic

"Open source" research is research conducted using only publicly-available information, although a paid subscription may be required to access a database containing the information. The most common form of research is to "Google" a topic or person, of course. If, for example, you wanted to find out how a competitor is approaching technically a new product they have announced, the "dream scenario" would be only a Google search and a few clicks away.

Assume for the sake of this example that your competitor has one of two options on approaching their new product technically, and that knowing how they are going about building their product will benefit your organization. Also assume that there will be new hiring to staff the development project. If the development project will involve recent graduates being hired, the chances of learning a great deal are high. Many graduate students have either their own home page or are listed on their department's home page, on which they will have at least the titles of their areas of research, if not the actual papers they have written as well as their thesis or dissertation. Simply reading the recent hire's papers could provide insight into your competitor's strategies.

But how would one be able to find out which organization hired the student in the first place? One way would be the department's home page, as it is useful for recruiting future students to let it be known the companies or government agencies attending the school's job fairs and where graduates find work after graduation. A second way would be the student's personal web page or blog, as they may contain a farewell message with where they will begin work after graduation. One Google search, for instance, allowed the author to find out that a particular consultancy his employer engages recently hired specialists in a particular area of expertise and that they place such a high value on objectivity that his new employer required all new employees to sign a several-page ethics statement promising to not allow any biases consciously influence their conclusions (the consultancy also has a rigorous review process for draft documents to further eliminate bias from creeping in unconsciously).

An Alternate Source Mosaic

There are, of course, less scrupulous means to gather information. The process for pretending to possess a legitimate need to know information when that is not the case is presented in a scenario adapted from Mitnick and Simon (2002).

The process for gathering the needed information takes place over the course of several phone calls. In the first call, an industry term to use when dealing with a particular service provider is confirmed under the guise of research for a book. A second call garnered the number the target company used to call the service provider when the perpetrator pretended to be an employee of the service provider verifying the number the target company uses to reach the provider. A third call then went to the service provider and the "researcher", armed with the special phone number, industry term and other information learned in the previous calls was able to obtain the information they wanted, in this case a credit history on a person they had been hired to investigate.

The subtlety of the operation lies in the relatively routine matters discussed in each individual call. The "I'm researching a book" excuse sounds great, but because it's now out in the open care should be taken to train employees to refuse to answer questions to unknown researchers. Should an employee encounter this situation, a policy should be in place that ensures they either refuse to answer, refer the caller to the media relations department if the organization has one, or at the very least take the name and number of the caller and inform their supervisor of the request before responding. The second call was disguised as a customer satisfaction survey in which one of the questions asked for the phone number used to reach the company. In this case, a supervisor should be notified. The third call was where the actual information the caller wanted was gathered. It would seem that this call doesn't have a defense unless a regularly-changed code is used to further authenticate the caller's right to the data. Aside from the rather unusual book research request, these calls would all appear to be within the normal course of a workday for those from whom the information was elicited. When taken together, an unauthorized credit check was run, possibly violating that person's privacy.

12.2 Social Engineering

Many readers will recognize the name "Mitnick" as Kevin Mitnick, the admitted criminal who used his powers of persuasion to gain access to various corporate and government networks, causing damages estimated in the millions of dollars. Now a security consultant, Mitnick helps organization protect against those who are now what he used to be. Mitnick claims to have never used his knowledge for ill, and he was pursued for having penetrated the networks illegally, but that is decidedly not the case for other hackers (the proper term is actually "cracker", but hacker has become the generic term to describe people who break into systems). The challenge to an organization is to understand the mentality of someone who would attempt to gain access to information they are not allowed to have.

12.2.1 The Mentality of a Successful Social Engineer

Like a successful poker player, a successful social engineer studies people and understands what they think and why. Like the flinty-eyed gambler, they use this knowledge to extract what they want (money or information) from their targets. In fact, "(t)ruly committed social engineers are better equated to actors and actresses rather than computer nerds. They read books about body language, voice control, vocal indicators and group dynamics. They study individual personality types that come out through body language and vocal cues, they practice observing these conscious and sub-conscious traits in others and themselves." (Lively, 2003)

Knowing where and how to strike is another consideration for a social engineer. Jones (2003) notes that there are three major physical areas in which an attack may occur.

The first area, the workplace, is discussed in the chapter on Physical Security as to policies and procedures recommended for handling the issue. Jones mentions "shoulder-surfing" passwords and door codes, as well as access to unlocked workstations connected to the organization's network or through unguarded network ports which may be accessed remotely after the attacker has left the area.

The second area is via the telephone. A scenario discussed above details how several telephone calls, each providing a bit of information needed to form a mosaic necessary to trick the ultimate target into revealing the desired information. Help desks, according to Jones, are a prime target, as it is their very job to help users who may not know very much about the system on which they're working. A successful social engineer must only create a reasonable enough scenario in which they've "messed up" their system to the point that they need the help desk customer service representative to give them the information they need to reset their system. A savvy social engineer will be able to tailor the call so the customer service representative will provide them the information they need to mount their attack over the natural course of the call. Because the incoming caller's number is often displayed on the recipient's phone, it would be necessary to "spoof" the local phone exchange or an internal operator to show the call as originating from an extension within the organization.

The third area Jones isolates is online. These attacks often occur via email (this is known as "phishing" and is discussed elsewhere) and Instant Messenger. In this mode of attack the victim is tricked into downloading malicious software onto their computer, allowing the bad guy (or girl) to do such things as track keystrokes, steal passwords or turn the target machine into a "zombie", launching spam emails.

A fourth area a social engineering attack may occur is in a place you frequent after work or take breaks during work. If you're a smoker, do you know everyone who's standing outside with you? How deeply do you and your colleagues delve into company strategy or technical details during happy hour, especially when it turns into a "happy couple of hours?" As silly as it sounds, the person sitting next to you could very well be pretending to concentrate on the ball game on the television while hoping to pick up any bit of information from your group. You simply never know, so it's best to avoid talking about work in any great detail in public, as difficult as that is to remember, because a person's natural tendency is to want to discuss such things with colleagues over a coffee or other beverage.

12.2.2 How a Social Engineer Uses What Your Parents Taught You to Their Advantage

For most Americans at least, we are taught as children to be friendly and helpful unless we're given a reason not to be. This is a very powerful psychological tendency a social engineer can exploit when dealing with us in any situation. Peltier (2006) lists the overarching factors impacting our likeliness to say "yes" to a social engineer:

- "The desire to be helpful." When customer service is the number one responsibility of an employee, and they are evaluated on the quality of service they provide, you must expect that if there is a doubt as to whether they will provide requested information or not, the default reaction will be to give it. Only through training and evaluation on not only positive feedback but the ability to recognize when *not* to provide information, through training and auditing strategies such as what is known in the telemarketing industry as "seeded calls", or calls in which the person on the other end of the line is hired by the organization for the sole purpose of trying to convince workers to not follow procedure and release information or take an unauthorized action.

- "A tendency to trust people." Basic American manners teach us to trust someone until they break their word. When someone tells us something we are trained to believe it unless we have evidence to the contrary. With a call coming from someone who sounds natural and uses the "lingo" appropriate to the situation, small irregularities will often be overlooked.

- "The fear of getting into trouble." A common tactic used by social engineers is to find out the name of a senior manager and when they will be out of the office. The ploy is then to call the employee and represent themselves as someone authorized by the manager who happens to be in an important meeting or if they're on vacation to have authorized them to call just before they left. Should the target of the scam refuse to give up the information, the next tactic is to threaten the employee with having their refusal to cooperate reported to their superior. If the person is convincing enough, they will often be able to force the victim to provide the information out of fear of being reprimanded or even fired. Finally,

- "The willingness to cut corners." As discussed elsewhere, employees adopt a level of effort they are able to sustain throughout the week to get them to the weekend. When a situation arises that could require a substantial amount of extra work, many people will choose to assume the person is legitimately asking for the information because it is more convenient to do so than to wait to visit the restroom, take a cigarette break or go home for the day.

As Peltier further notes, the real problem with social engineers is that the truly accomplished ones never arouse any suspicion; it's only the clumsy or less-talented scammers that get caught.

12.3 Countering the Social Engineer

The way to fight back against the social engineer is obvious: establish policies that make the organization resistant to the wiles of scammers through training, methods to test employee vigilance and real implications for employees found to have not behaved with appropriate rigor when confronted with a social engineer.

12.3.1 Awareness

While training is addressed elsewhere in this book, the need for it is felt directly when considering the social engineering threat. Ultimately it is the role of people, not technology to provide the last line of defense against theft. In many expert opinions, awareness is the first place to spend money (Britt, 2005). The physical security steps were covered in its own chapter; please refer to them as well.

Some information should never be revealed over the phone under any but the most specific circumstances. As time has passed, fewer and fewer organizations are printing copies of their phone directories, because having them at the ready could tell you, depending on how detailed the information it contains is, how the organization is structured. Another bit of information that can be used is the "accidental wrong number." In this ruse, the scammer dials the last digit of a phone number incorrectly and apologizes to the person who answers, but then asks if they would walk down the hall and get the information they want from the target. The unknowing participant would likely think they're simply helping someone out, and the target would be giving the information to a co-worker they see every day. Because of this, not only should phone directories not be published, but policies stopping this kind of information sharing should be prohibited. Examples of types of information that should never be revealed include passwords, company-specific terms, computer names and port numbers. (Erlanger, 2005) Ensuring all employees are properly aware through multiple media helps maintain an appropriate alert level.

12.3.2 Auditing

The term "auditing" is typically associated with accounting, but applies here as well, in that a review of security policies should occur at reasonable intervals. It's impractical to try to recommend a standard time span between audits, but a general rule is to constantly monitor known threats and see how the written policies counter them. At times, only a few policies may need to be updated. Other times, whole sections or the entire document will need to be revised. As this book was researched, new threats that had barely been mentioned came to prominence and others became decidedly "behind the times".

A second type of auditing is staged attempts to execute social engineering missions on the target organization. Orgil, et al (2004), describe a project in which a young, technically savvy (read "stereotypical computer room geek") was able to gain access to an organization's facility and networks through social engineering. They may also be engaged to attempt social engineering over the phone. These phone calls should be recorded and the results used for training purposes only, unless the employee displays blatant carelessness or other patently inappropriate behavior. Should the possibility of these calls exist, all employees should be aware of it. If nothing else, there should be a strong deterrent effect when they know the person on the other end of the line may be trying to trick them while their supervisors are listening.

12.4 Relevant Policies

Ultimately, because workers are constantly trying to get through their day while doing a good job and not making any mistakes, it is important to remember that policies take for granted an employee's good intentions. Bluntly, don't assume that they are lazy and don't care about the organization's needs and potential legal liabilities. Even though this will be true for some (hopefully small) percentage of the workers, the majority will try to do the right thing out of a sense of professionalism if nothing else. With that in mind, some recommended policies are adapted from Peltier (2005) and Jones (2003)

- Unattended workstations must be locked. For the intruder who has made it into the facility the first target is a computer that running without the locking screen saver activated. At this point, the interloper is, to the network, the legitimate user. Security personnel should, at random times, walk around the work area to see if any workstations are left unattended and unlocked. A rule of thumb is that if the security officer can't see the user while standing by the workstation or then they should have locked it. Another test would be for the security officer to have an operation to perform on the machine that would take approximately the time a currently popular form of attack requires. An employee violating this should be re-trained at first, but more severe sanctions should result if they continue to not follow procedures. As an organization's pay grades will likely be a function of the importance of a job, following security policies should be a formal part of the employee's performance review.

- Written passwords should not be left lying out. Because employees have many different passwords for many different systems, many with the "at least one number and at least one special character" requirement, it is no longer practical to assume that an individual will be able to memorize all of their authentication details. What is important now is that the location of where they are written down is kept secret. Apparently, for example, some people still put their passwords on a sticky note and affix it somewhere on their computer or desk. Only slightly more deceptive is when they put the sticky note on the underside of their keyboard. Good places to keep copies of passwords are:
  - o Computer files named something other than "password" or "log-in",
  - o A small piece of paper kept in a wallet or purse, and
  - o In fake addresses in one's contact manager.
- Employees should not be overburdened. In the end, while security is a critical part of an employee's job, it is in fact *not* their primary responsibility. This should always be remembered. Should employees feel like their being treated as if they have already or will have soon given away the "crown jewels", they may react negatively by defying the security policy mandates or looking for other jobs. An inability to do one's job because of excessive security procedures could also decrease a worker's satisfaction, and as such a key balance must be struck between vigilance and ability to comply.
- What to do when an attack is detected should be well defined. Each employee should be trained on how to handle an incident. A checklist should be developed and distributed. For easy reference, each employee should keep their checklist prominently

displayed on their desk, right? Wrong! Should an intruder get into the facility, it would be simple to grab a copy of the checklist and make off with it. At that point, a strategy can be developed to counter the steps they know will be taken in case they are suspected of being a social engineer.

Finally, while it's always best to stress the positive aspects of the role an employee plays in protecting an organization, it is necessary to be firm in the sanctions to be imposed in case of unauthorized release of confidential information. Demotions, transfer to lower-paying positions not requiring the handling of confidential information and even termination are possible consequences.

12.5 Applying the Balanced Scorecard to the Human Element

The goals and their measures in establishing a reference Human Element balanced scorecard are:

Goal: Ensure the organization understands which information it possesses that is valuable and how it could be acquired.

- Information is properly classified.
  - o In each employee's executing their normal duties, what do they do? With whom do they interact? Is the business process documented? How long ago was this last updated?
  - o Have the different ways the information each employee has access to could be used been documented? When taken in isolation and in combination, what picture does the information create? How long ago was the last documentation?
- Enhance the organization's awareness of its information exposure.
  - o What information is available about the organization and its employees on the organization's web site? What information is available via employees' personal web logs or web pages? How often are routine searches conducted?
  - o Have the sources and methods available to open-source researchers and social engineers been incorporated into the security awareness program? When was the training material last updated?

Goal: Understand how a social engineer could penetrate the organization and collect confidential information.

- Protect the sources of confidential information within the organization
  - o Are the phones of those who provide confidential information reachable directly from outside the organization? Are the phone numbers available on the internet? When was the last audit conducted?
  - o Are employees regularly asked about how they would go about collecting confidential information if they were a social engineer? How often is "refresher training" conducted?
- Ensure employees are exercising the appropriate diligence in protecting the organization.
  - o Are employees aware of how to deal with suspected social engineering attacks?
    - ▪ What percentage of employees are trained in recognizing social engineering attacks?
    - ▪ How often is refresher training conducted?
  - o Are audits, such as calls from persons hired by the organization to test the system, performed regularly?
    - ▪ How long ago was the last "seeded call" to a staff member placed?
    - ▪ How many violations were reported during the last period of measure?

12.6 Summary

The role of human beings in protecting an organization is complex and filled with uncertainties. A normally diligent worker could have a lapse in judgment resulting from being distracted by problems at home, illness or a heavy workload. Workers who are marginally diligent could become lazy and willing to cut corners in order to not have to delay a break or going home for the day. Social engineers prey upon these people; and the larger and busier an organization is the more likely a determined penetration team will eventually succeed, as its members will continue to try to access the needed information over and over again until they finally succeed. Great care should be taken and thorough pre-screening, training and auditing of employees entrusted with confidential information should always occur.

12.7 Discussion Questions

In your organization, what kind of information is available to someone
- On the internet?
- In general marketing material?
- In government filings, such as with the Securities and Exchange Commission?
- In the trade press?
- In employee personal web sites and web logs?

If a social engineer were to communicate with someone at the help desk or with the section of your organization from which confidential data is communicated routinely, would they have a specific technical vocabulary they would need to have mastered in order to be seen as "routine" traffic?
- What are the terms?
- Are these terms readily available in books, journals or on the internet?
- Is there anything about your organization's security regime that would prevent someone calling the correct number, using the correct technical terms effortlessly and asking for routine information that would prevent it from being given to an unauthorized party?

What are some possible implications of your organization's information falling into unauthorized hands?
- Personal privacy violations?
- Transactional data?
- Intellectual property?

Chapter 13 Email, Instant Messaging and Phishing

Chapter Objectives

This chapter will discuss:
- The role email and instant messaging (IM) play in our daily work lives,
- How email has become part of regulatory compliance and legal discovery processes,
- Future trends in managing email,
- IM's prevalence among the rising generation of employees,
- Trends in IM threats,
- Suggested IM policies,
- Phishing and its definition,
- The shocking success of increasingly sophisticated phishing attacks, and
- Means and resources for combating phishers.

13.1 Email and Instant Messaging are Crucial but Vulnerable

It is certainly unnecessary to explain to those reading this book the importance real-time and near real-time communication have in a modern organization's ability to function effectively. Because many who must work with each other are not able to conduct business face-to-face, and playing "phone tag" is far less of an option now because of the time constraints on operations in today's environment. Two of the means for communication, email and Instant Messaging (IM) have become targets for mischievous and criminal minds. Through clever means such as "phishing", which is discussed in this chapter, pranksters, hucksters and mobsters are finding more and more clever ways to trick the user into downloading a malignant file or clicking on a URL that will load a piece of malware on the user's machine. It is essential that both these dangers and the requirements to retain documents be understood. Email will be discussed first, then IM and finally phishing and its dangers will be covered.

13.2 Email

As was noted in Chapter 1, Morgan Stanley was found to be negligent in their non-production of emails demanded by investor Ron Perelman during a fraud lawsuit. To avoid this and compliance issues, such as Sarbanes-Oxley concerns, an organization should implement a system that manages email sufficiently to avoid running afoul of such requirements.

13.2.1 Managing Email

One organization, Open Text (reported in Rabe, 2005), has developed an "E-mail Management Framework" to guide organizations in their meeting Email retention requirements. The framework is based on three levels:

- Storage,
- Manage, and
- Comply.

As this framework comes from a knowledge management perspective, the storage capabilities involve bringing emails from the email server to a storage device automatically, which is able to retain more emails more efficiently while maintaining the ability to find the messages in a manner which complies with archiving standards in regulated industries while allowing workers to go about their business normally.

The manage capability supports legal discovery and "structured retention management" of the organization's emails. The capabilities are:

- "Full Text Search- Information retrieval capabilities based on a proven search engine.
- "Journaling- Journaling capabilities are coupled with a powerful records management backend, which enables centrally captured information to be used for records management purposes.
- "Retention and Disposition- Organizations need to be able to retrieve e-mail documents at a moment's notice and manage the process of their destruction when it is legally permissible to do so. The manage layer provides the ability to control both the retention and destruction of e-mails.

- "Auditing- Powerful auditing functionality tracks actions that are performed on objects in the archive repository. An audit trail identifies and describes the type of operation performed on the item, the date and time of the operation and the user who performed the operation.
- "Legal discovery- The manage layer fully supports legal discovery processes by utilizing indexing, searching, offline exporting of search results and auditing capabilities." (Rabe, 2005)

Finally, the comply functionality helps the organization meet the requirements of such requirements as HIPAA.

13.2.2 Future Trends in Email

Email is a well-established communication and collaboration tool for all levels of workers in an organization. Because of its popularity, it is has become the "attack vector" for seemingly innumerable attempts to send spam or to attempt to steal information, among other things. Anthes (2006) recently wrote about three key trends for email.

First, his interviews established that while the amount of unwanted email and attacks are quite high now, technology and other factors will serve to mitigate the malicious attacks. Ray Tomlinson, the first person to send a network email in history, has termed the battle "pretty much a draw" to this point, and feels that the business and political will to take decisive action against the problem will eventually catch up with the technical ability to stop it, which he feels is currently good enough to succeed.

Vendors are beginning to develop products designed to fight the spread of spam and phishing messages. For example, Microsoft has developed the Sender ID Framework, which "verifies that a message was actually sent from a server authorized to send mail for the domain owner." (ibid) In addition, Yahoo! and Cisco have jointly submitted their Domain Keys Identified Mail proposed standard to the Internet Engineering Task Force (IETF). As of this writing, a formal Request for Comment (RFC) had yet to be published but a working group had been chartered. The standard, according to Libbey (2006), who is with Yahoo!, works as follows:

- "The sending domain publishes a public key in its DNS record,
- "The sending mail server digitally signs and sends the message,

- "The receiving mail server retrieves the public key from the sending domain's DNS record. It verifies the digital signature using the message content and the key, and
- "The receiving mail server delivers the e-mail to the end user's mailbox."

Microsoft has completed an experimental version of a spam defense called SmartProof. As it currently works:

- "A machine-learning filter...snags the obvious spam and quarantines it or throws it away. The filter passes on to the user's in-box any message that is from someone on the user's 'whitelist,'
- "Messages suspected of being spam trigger replies to the senders, challenging them to prove they're not spammers,
- "Senders may respond to the challenge by solving some kind of puzzle—one that's easy for a human but hard for an automatic spam generator, or
- "Alternately, senders can ensure the delivery of their messages by making credit card-based 'micropayments.' The payments may go to the receipient, the Internet service provider or a charity, or they can be refunded to the sender if the message turns out not to be spam." (Anthes, 2006)

> **Important:** The examples provided above are intended solely to whet the appetite of the reader to research the topic further. There are without a doubt several solid examples of research projects in the field that are not a part of a major corporate effort, which could be a better "fit" for the reader's organization or could provide further insight into the matter to allow the organization to make a fully informed choice should one of the two options mentioned in the above discussion be adopted.

In addition, "Microsoft has identified some seventy or so types of file extensions that it believes could harbor dangerous executable content designed to take advantage of buffer overflows and compromise (one's) system." File extensions on the 'danger list' include:

- .bat—Microsoft batch file
- .cmd—Command file for Windows NT

- .scr—Screen saver (portable executable file)
- .vb—Visual Basic file
- .wsf—Windows script file (Musthaler, 2006)

Second, Anthes notes that email is likely going to remain the dominant communication medium for the foreseeable future. As discussed in other parts of the book, however, the real issue will come in areas of communication less able to be controlled, such as employee blogs. IBM Research has recently prototyped a collaboration tool named Activity Explorer that "pulls together e-mail messages, synchronous communication such as instant messages, screen images, files, folders and to-do lists," and "Microsoft Research has developed a way to combine e-mail, files, Web pages, calendar entries, to-do-lists and other materials into one searchable archive" known as "Stuff I've Seen." (ibid)

Third is the evolution of applications turning email inboxes into knowledge management repositories. In many organizations designated knowledge management applications aren't used even when company policy makes their use mandatory. The result is that each employee's inbox becomes the repository of the "latest and greatest" versions of documents, presentations and collaboration patterns. According to HP researcher Bernardo Huberman "(y)ou can look at an organizational chart and make all sorts of inferences about how people work, but when you look at e-mail patterns, you see how they work in a different way. You discover leadership roles, such as who's the hub through which most of the e-mails go, that you wouldn't identify from the organizational chart." (Anthes, 2006)

> **Important:** One method to consider when performing business process reengineering is to see perform an analysis of email traffic (known as "social network analysis") to see how business processes are accomplished in practice versus what the formal organization chart of business process flow diagram depicts. It can also be informative in defining the "hubs" through which information flows as well as those who may be in a position of authority but are in fact avoided whenever possible.

13.2.3 Email in Summary

The basic utility of email is now well-known. The follow-on issue as identified in the literature discussed in this section is how to take email and turn it into a useable medium for more than informal communication while at the same time eliminating the inconvenience and outright jeopardy presented by those who wish to use it as an attack vector for their own purposes. Ultimately, email and IM are discoverable in legal and audit proceedings, so all organizations would do well to investigate what is actually being communicated through email over the organization's networks.

13.3 Instant Messaging

Instant Messaging (IM) has risen to prominence in a relatively short time. To the eyes of many, in the U.S. at least, the early adopters for IM were adolescents and pre-adolescents, who used IM as a way to stay in touch with friends before the days of mobile phone plans with unlimited or virtually unlimited usage at reasonable prices. As these children, discussed extensively by Tapscott (1997), learned to communicate with each other, they were able to leverage the new technology of IM and email rather than needing to tie up the family phone line all the time (although they still managed to do so, as well as amassing sometimes shocking mobile phone bills).

As these children have become old enough to join the workforce and as older people have also adopted IM as a tool, it is now common to "chat" with several different people at the same time. For organizations in which quick feedback and judgments are required, IM is a wonderful tool. A major drawback to IM is that because of its traditionally informal nature, when it is used in a business setting those communicating with it may forget that what they are "saying" is capturable and can be used as evidence in audit and legal proceedings, such as a case in which Yahoo! alleged that some of its former employees used IM to "distribute confidential business and technical data for use with their new employer, a competing startup. Records of this IM correspondence became a key piece of evidence in the case" (Newsfactor.com, 2006). Some organizations have banned its use on organization computers, but there are now so many ways to access IM that it is likely that no matter what the policy a way to use IM will be found.

One way in which organizations are protecting themselves against improper disclosures is through random monitoring of IM in the same way customer service calls are monitored. In fact:

> "Call centers recognized this long ago, when they started recording calls at random for 'auditing' and 'training' pur-

poses. Once these policies were implemented, the quality and compliance to corporate policy dramatically increased. Establishing an IM policy and reminding employees that monitoring tools are in place can go a long way in averting potential problems down the road." (ibid)

13.3.1 IM Threat Trends

IM's surge in popularity has led to it being identified as a good attack vector for hackers. One of the favorite infections of IM attackers, the worm, is highly resistant to being detected by traditional software, which is compounded by the fact that they often mutate, as the traditional anti-virus software is reactive, in that it searches for already-identified attacks. Because IM is a conduit for the rapid dissemination of attacks through a user's contact list (see the end of the section for a list of relevant IM terms). Even more worrisome is that threats are able to make the transition across networks as well as from public networks to internal ones. (IM-Logic Threat Center, 2005 in Review, 2006) Five top risks have also been identified.

First, rapid adoption and improved interoperability of are going to lead to an ever-increasing number of IM threats. IM threats increased by almost 1700% in 2005, and given what is expected to be an environment with even more participants and users there is no indication that the amount of jeopardy IM users face will decrease.

Second, IM is moving from a strictly text-based medium to one that supports Voice Over Internet Protocol (VOIP) and even conferencing. As voice and chat functionalities merge, there will be even more paths for an attacker to use to attempt to compromise a target system.

Third, worms are becoming ever more sophisticated. One quite impressive example is the "talking worm," which engages the target in conversation.

Fourth, criminals will continue to see IM as a good target. IM has been established as a very effective avenue for spreading malware, and hardened criminals are the ones designing the threats rather than those looking to spread mischief rather than mayhem. Spam over IM (SPIM), is also becoming more common, as it is a simple matter to "spoof" an organization's identity in a believable way, which is also a good way to launch a successful phishing attack, as will be discussed later in the chapter.

Finally, IM is a conduit for losing intellectual property, as IM can be used as a file transfer mechanism. Because file size is usually not restricted over IM, while it may well be over an email network; content filters don't likely exist; and the desire to keep some transactions a secret, IM is an ideal "workaround" for avoiding what an organization would like to control. The way to counter this, of course, is to enact policies mandating that IM communication be monitored and that an employee has been notified that any messages they make regarding work could be subject to monitoring and archiving. (ibid)

13.3.2 Recommended IM Policies

There are four policy points recommended to be followed in determining how to approach IM within an organization.

First, it is essential to determine the extent to which IM is currently in use within the organization. IM is still a new enough technology that many organizations have not yet assessed its impact on how IM is used to execute its business processes. Auditing usage will show who is using IM and with whom they are communicating.

Second, a strategy on how to protect the organization from specific IM threats may be developed. As is logical, the most significant threats should be identified and protected against first. After the current threats have been identified and countered, attention may turn to assessing the risk of future attacks as well as remaining vigilant to determine how well the defense against older attacks is continuing to function.

Third, a policy codifying acceptable IM use should be developed and implemented. Users should be trained as to the acceptable and unacceptable uses of IM with regard to the organization and the policy should be monitored to ensure it is being followed.

Fourth, after the immediate need of developing and implementing a baseline acceptable use policy has been met, the next stage should be to determine the best direction for a long-term IM strategy for the organization. As IM technologies mature, becoming more functional, interoperable and economical, how its use as a collaboration tool will evolve should be watched closely. (IMLogic Threat Center, *Managing Instant Messaging for Business Advantage*; 2006)

13.3.3 Key IM Policy Elements

A list of significant terms to be referenced in formulating a policy is included in Figure 13.1.

IM Usage Policy Components

Subject   A concise title for the policy, such as "Instant Messaging Usage Policy."

Purpose   A single, simple sentence stating the overarching goal of the policy. If it is the first version of the policy, the sentence could start with the words "To establish." If it is a follow-on version, it may be worded "To renew," "To replace," or "To update" the previous policy.

Guidelines   A statement identifying all covered by the policy, including identifiers such as "all organizational employees" or "all who use the organization's network(s)."

Acceptable Use   When using IM while connected to the organization's network, whether for business or personal communication, all guidelines as to content, disallowed sites and other acceptable uses such as those found in the email policy shall also be followed.

Ownership   Any IM correspondence transmitted over the organization's networks is the sole property of the organization.

Personal   Personal IM is/is not allowed over the organization's networks. If it is allowed, it should not be excessive and should not interfere with the organization's functioning.

Privacy   An employee should expect that any IM usage on the organization's network is subject to monitoring and thus has no right to privacy regarding IM.

Discovery   IM is subject to discovery in legal proceedings and regulatory compliance audits. As such, any IM traffic over the organization's network may be provided to outside parties authorized to receive it.

Conduct   Each organization should have a policy mandating proper conduct at all time to include not creating messages that are offensive, of a sexual nature, harassing, and so on. This also prohibits transmitting proprietary information and other business-related objectives.

Signature   Each employee should sign the policy document acknowledging that they have read, understand and will abide by the policy.

Passwords   Password policies for IM should be the same as they are for network and email accounts.

IM Apps   Because of the risk of malware being spread through IM downloads, audio, video and games shall not be downloaded over IM. In addition, only authorized IM applications (MSN, AOL, for example) are allowed to be used.

Penalties   Should the policy be violated, various disciplinary measures may be taken at the sole discretion of the organization. These may include: verbal warning, counseling and retraining, loss of IM privileges, suspension and termination.

Figure 13.1 IM Acceptable Use Concepts (adapted from IMLogic Threat Center, *Managing Instant Messaging for Business Advantage*, 2006)

IM is very popular communication medium, but with its convenience comes the ability for those with malicious intent to exploit IM for their own gain. In addition to policies to protect the organization's network from a technical perspective, the concepts above provide the baseline on which to base a user-based IM policy.

13.4 Phishing

Phishing, as in "fishing," adapted to mimic the spelling used in "phone phreaking," the exploitation of telephone networks in the pre-World Wide Web era, is "a form of online fraud that has exploded in frequency over the last several years. Typically using large-volume email campaigns, Phishers try to trick people into sharing personal information that the thieves then sell or use to commit identity theft." (Hines, 2005)   In the past, it would manifest itself mostly in the type of email shown in Figure 13.2. There are several plainly evident problems with the message.

First, the grammar and spelling are very bad. Those accustomed to dealing with non-native speakers know that while perfect fluency is not a realistic expectation, it should be better than what is in this message if the real goal is to solicit serious business opportunities.

Second, there is no address listed in the "To" field. This should raise alarms instantly, as while bulk mailings are easy to see, as it is when the recipient is the sender and the bulk list is then put on a "bcc:" ("blind carbon copy," for those of you young enough to have never used carbon paper to make a copy on a manual typewriter) line.

Third, the writer attempts to induce the receiver to release enough information (full name, address, occupation) to likely enable the phisher to steal the receiver's identify.

From: "Major Biz Ltd" majorbizltd101@lycos.co.uk
Subject: BUSINESS PATNER NEEDED!!

Date: Wed, 21 Jun 2006 00:06:37 +0200

To:

Dear Sir/Madam,
I am Mr. Abdiel Andree Lee. I work with group of business men who
deal on raw materials such as Calcite, Barytes, Manganese, Dioxide,
Dolomite, Mica, China Clay ,Mangnese and Construction chemicals.
Our Company(Major Biz INT'L) was established in 1991.Over the years
we have accumulated invaluable experience in our business and we
are proud to claim we are first among equals.

 We have limited countries where our products are been exported.Due
to the quality of our products we have some successfully few
customers in America and Canada Countries...

By so doing, we are searching for reliable persons/companies who can
act as DISTRIBUTOR/RECEIVING OFFICER for us...

If aprroved as our Representative,you are entitled to an annual income
of $25,000USD and 10% of whatever amount you receive from
customers who are making payments through you to us.Please if you
are interested in transacting business with Us, we will be very glad.
Please, forward to us the following informations,

> 1. Full Names.....
> 2. House Address......
> 3. Phone Number.....
> 4. State.....
> 5. Country......
> 6. Occupation......

(Email contact invited to a yahoo.com.cn address, no phone number
provided.)

Figure 13.2 Actual Suspected Phishing Email

Important: This example is an amateurish attempt to collect information. As will be discussed below, the techniques being used are becoming much more sophisticated.

13.4.1 Phishing Becomes More Sophisticated

While most people would easily recognize the email from Figure 13.2 as fraudulent, the scam artists are becoming better and better at developing convincing attacks. According to one expert, "technology is the rising tide that lifts all ships, including pirate ships." (Wetzel, 2005) What is worse is that phishers are working in teams, as opposed to the typical "lone wolf" virus writer. (Millard, 2005) In fact, the success rates seen by expert observers are "amazing," in that people expecting to see the type of email shown above fall victim to a more sophisticated attack, some of which are including correct information of the intended target. (Hines, 2005)

One of the new wave of phishing scams attacked U.S. credit unions with the hope of tricking the users into clicking on a link to site that then attempted to install two programs on the victim's machine. The message, "though poorly worded, was well-targeted to bank administrators, and Hudson Valley (Credit Union) had a number of employees who clicked on the URL in the message." It was reported that the credit union's defenses stopped the malware from actually making it onto the credit union's machines, but the fact the employees did click on the link demonstrates the attacks' effectiveness. (Roberts, 2005)

A second type of phishing emails includes *correct account information,* "including the customer's name, email address and full account number. The messages are crafted to appear as if they have been sent by the banks in order to verify other account information, such as an ATM personal identification number or a credit card CVD code, a series of digits printed on the back of most cards as an extra form of identification." (Hines, 2005) Wetzel (2005) notes another type of scam email which states that the customer's account will be cancelled unless they go to a website and verify their credit card number, PIN and perhaps other bits of information. The data is collected, the website is taken down, and the data is sold to a third party for their use.

Because of the success of phishing emails, they will not be going away any time soon. The Anti-Phishing Working Group released a report on the number and types of attacks. The details are found in Figure 13.3.

Highlights

- Number of unique phishing reports received in May: 20,109
- Number of unique phishing sites received in May: 11,976
- Number of brands hijacked by phishing campaigns in May: 137
- Number of brands comprising the top 80% of phishing campaigns in May: 20
- Country hosting the most phishing websites in May: United States
- Contain some form of target name in URL: 46 %
- No hostname just IP address: 42 %
- Percentage of sites not using port 80:   8 %
- Average time online for site: 5.0 days
- Longest time online for site: 31 days

Figure 13.3 Phishing Attack Report for May, 2006 (source: Anti-Phishing Working Group, 2006)

> **Important:** Port 80 is the port that a server "listens to" for data from the Web client when the client is default configured, but another, single, port may be used. (www.bytepile.com, 2006)

Of particular concern is the massive number of unique phishing reports and number of unique phishing sites received solely in May, 2006. In addition, it is perhaps surprising that the United States is the country hosting the most phishing websites. In fact, the strong plurality (34.1%) is hosted in the U.S. Figure 13.4 shows the top ten countries hosting phishing websites.

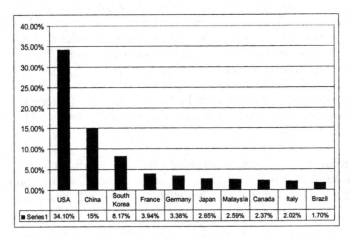

	USA	China	South Korea	France	Germany	Japan	Malaysia	Canada	Italy	Brazil
■ Series1	34.10%	15%	8.17%	3.94%	3.38%	2.65%	2.59%	2.37%	2.02%	1.70%

Figure 13.4 Countries Hosting Phishing Sites (Adapted from Anti-Phishing Working Group, 2006)

Financial services is by far the most targeted industry, at 92% of total phishing expeditions. Internet Service Providers (3.6%) and Retail (1.5%) are the next most targeted, with Miscellaneous ("Other") sectors being targeted 3.6% of the time. (Anti-Phishing Working Group, 2006)

The average time for a site to actually exist was less than one week, which means the phishing scammers are very serious about the "hit and run" method of operations. It is worth noting that phishing is having a real impact on consumer confidence in one's ability to bank online securely. In 2004, a survey of several hundred banking customers found that "65 percent of account holders were less likely to use their bank's online services due to phishing, and 75 percent were less likely to respond to email from their bank because of phishing." (Wetzel, 2005)

13.4.2 A Study on Phishing

A recent study conducted by Dhamija, et al (2006), demonstrates the troubling effectiveness of a particular method of phishing. Among other websites, the authors created a fake website spoofing Bank of the West to cause the participants to mistakenly identify the site as legitimate rather than recognizing it for what it was. Because web users have become more sophisticated, "successful phishers must not only present a high-credibility presence to their victims; they must create a presence that is so impressive that it causes the victim to fail to recognize security measures installed in web browsers." (ibid)

In this case, the authors replicated a website for Bank of the West (Sturgeon, 2006). The URL was:

www.bankofthevvest.com

You very likely noticed that the spoofed website URL has a "double v" as opposed to a "w" in its makeup. Because you're reading this book you are very likely more aware than most of the techniques phishers use to trick their victims into providing desired information. But how well would you do if you didn't have the contextual guide of knowing you are reading a chapter on, among other things, phishing?

As it turns out, the participants in the Dhamija, et al study (2006) did not fare very well at all. For this particular spoofed website, which included a fake padlock like the one seen in the bottom right corner of the screen when on a secure connection, a fake VeriSign logo and seal, and a pop-up security alert, fully 91 percent of users indicated they thought the site was legitimate. (Sturgeon, 2006) In fact:

- "Good phishing websites fooled 90% of participants.
- "Existing anti-phishing browsing cues are ineffective. 23% of participants in (the) study did not look at the address bar, status bar, or the security indicators.
- "On average, our participant group made mistakes on our test set 40% of the time.
- "Popup warnings about fraudulent certificates were ineffective: 15 out of 22 participants proceeded without hesitation when presented with warnings.
- "Participants proved vulnerable across the board to phishing attacks. In our study, neither education, age, sex, previous experience, nor hours of computer use showed a statistically significant correlation with vulnerability to phishing." (Dhamija, et al, 2006)

> **Important:** While this study involved only 22 participants and can't be generalized to internet users as a whole, the results showing no reliable indicator of vulnerability to phishing should be a major cause for concern. Only properly trained and vigilant workers who are aware of the possible implications for the organization and themselves if they were to fall victim to a social engineering or phishing scam and release proprietary or otherwise protected information should be allowed to staff those important positions. This is a repetition of material in Chapter 12, but the potential losses to the organization are so significant that it is worth re-emphasizing.

13.5 Fighting the Phishers

So, the question becomes, how does one protect against the phishing threat? Taken together, Wetzel (2005) and Dhamija, et al (2006) offer the following suggested policies:

Recognize when a secure connection (https:// rather than http://) is in use. This signifies that the traffic is being transmitted over SSL/TLS (Secure Sockets Layer and Transport Layer Security). When SSL/TLS is used, that the server from which the information is being requested has a *certificate*, or a digital "signature" that provides the identity of the issuer. Some organizations sign their own certificates, but those certificates should generate a warning message, as would an expired certificate. The best certificate is one that has been signed by a *Certificate Authority*. A list of trusted Certificate Authorities is stored in the browser, as those with relatively less rigor will run the risk of issuing certificates to fraudulent sites. When implemented properly, however, mutual authentication established through certificate exchange issued by trusted Certificate Authorities ensures as well as possible that the information being transmitted is coming from and being received by parties who are in fact who they claim to be.

> **Important:** Social Engineering and Phishing rely on the ability to trick the intended victim that the fraudster requesting the information is authorized to receive it. Certificates from trusted Certificate Authorities help substantially mitigate the chance that anything "phishy" is taking place.

Provide spam filtering. Email is currently the most common avenue of attack, and a strong anti-spam filter helps prevent spam emails from being delivered. When successful, the intended victim never has the opportunity to mistakenly release the information.

> **Important:** Neither training nor technology by themselves are going to decrease the risk of unauthorized disclosure as much as the two methods working together. It will likely cost more to do both training and technology, but that will pale in comparison to the risk the organization will run if it takes only one or neither of the steps.

Detect Domain Name Infringement: As noted by Sturgeon (2006), it is possible to register domain names, such as www.bankofthevvest.com versus www.bankofthewest.com, which so closely resemble the legitimate URL that it is understandable that some small percentage of users will be tricked into providing their information to the imitator. By tracking new domain names as they are registered, organizations will be able to know when possible scam-enabling sites are established and should then take all legal steps necessary to ensure the site is taken down.

13.6 List of Potential Vendors

Wetzel (2005) provided a list of potential anti-phishing vendors. Those with websites are included below:

41st Parameter (www.41stparameter.com)
Bharosa (www.bharosa.com)
Billeo (www.billeo.com)
BioPassword (www.biopassword.com)
Corillian (www.corillian.com)
Cyota (www.cyota.com)
Cyveillance (www.cyveillance.com)
Digital Envoy (www.digitalenvoy.com)
EarthLink (www.earthlink.com)
Entrust (www.entrust.com)
Envisional (www.envisional.com)
GeoTrust (www.geotrust.com)
Goodmail (www.goodmail.com)
Ironport (www.ironport.com)
MarkMonitor (www.markmonitor.com)
McAfee (www.mcafee.com)
Microsoft (www.microsoft.com)
NameProtect (www.nameprotect.com)
Netcraft (www.netcraft.com)
PassMark (www.passmark.com)
PhishFree (www.phishfree.com)
Postini (www.postini.com)
Real User (www.realuser.com)
RSA (www.rsasecurity.com)
SafeScrypt (www.safescrypt.com)
ShareCube (www.sharecube.com)
Symantec (www.symantec.com)
Vasco Data Security (www.vasco.com)
VeriSign (www.verisign.com)
Webroot Software (www.webroot.com)
WholeSecurity (www.wholesecurity.com)

13.7 Applying the Balanced Scorecard to Email, Instant Messaging and Phishing

The goals and their measures in establishing a reference Executive Communication balanced scorecard are:

Goal: Ensure the organization's email is controlled properly.

- Does the email server automatically transfer emails to a storage device, enabling compliant archiving while not interfering with the normal flow of business? How long ago was the system last tested?
- Does the email management capability support legal discovery through "structured retention management"?
    - o Does the system allow for full text search, rather than simply by subject? How long ago was the system last tested?
    - o Does a "journaling" capability couple with a records management capability? What percentage of records requiring accompanying journal entries had them?
    - o Are emails retained in such a way as to be readily available should the need to produce them arise?
        - ▪ How long ago was the system last tested?
        - ▪ What percentage of emails were retrieved successfully?
    - o Does the system allow for auditing to include:
        - ▪ Type of operation performed,
        - ▪ Date and time of the operation, and
        - ▪ User who performed the operation?
        - ▪ How long ago was the auditing function last tested?
    - o Does the system support legal discovery through:
        - ▪ Indexing,
        - ▪ Searching,
        - ▪ Offline exporting search results, and
        - ▪ Auditing?
        - ▪ How long ago was a simulated legal discovery test undertaken?
- Does the system enable compliance with regulations such as Sarbanes-Oxley and HIPAA? How long ago was the system's compliance capability last validated?

- Does the email system have a strong and updated spam filter? How often is the filter updated?
- Is the email system able to be leveraged as or by a knowledge management/business intelligence application? What is the satisfaction level of users performing sample or real KM/BI activities?

Goal: Ensure the organization's instant messaging (IM) is controlled properly.

- Has the amount of business transacted over IM by those within your organization been determined?
  - o How many people and in which departments use IM to conduct organizational business? How long ago was this usage level last validated?
  - o What is the nature of the information communicated over IM? How long ago was the last audit performed?
- Has a "threat matrix" of known and anticipated attack techniques been developed?
  - o How is the organization monitoring existing and emerging threats? How long ago was the methodology last validated?
  - o Has the impact of VOIP use to have "phone" conversations been evaluated? How many calls are placed inappropriately over VOIP to discuss business?
- Has a policy delineating acceptable IM use been implemented? How long ago was it last updated?
- Has a procedure for updating the IM (and all technology-related policies, for that matter) been developed?
  - o Is a procedure in place to monitor the evolution of IM technologies? How long ago was it last updated?
  - o Is a procedure in place to update the IM usage policies on a regular basis? How long ago was it last updated?

Goal: Ensure the organization's employees are trained adequately to detect and resist phishing attacks.

- Are employees instructed to report/forward suspected phishing emails to IT security? How many reportable incidents have not been reported?

- Have phishing attacks been identified within your industry that use information specific to it or even that use a person's unique information? How long does it take for a new phishing attack to appear before your organization is aware of it?
- Is a training regimen in place to help users identify phishing attacks? How long ago was the last training held?
- Is technology in place to filter out as many phishing emails as possible? How long ago was the filter last updated?
- Are new domain name registrations being monitored to know when a site mimicking your organization's URL has been established? How long ago were the domain name registries last searched?
- Is there a procedure in place to report and remediate, if necessary, a suspected unauthorized information release? How long ago was the policy last updated?
- Are the organization's senior executives trained to identify phishing attacks? If the executives have Administrative Assistants or what in military terms would be termed Executive Officers, are they trained to do the same? How long ago were the senior executives last trained to identify phishing attacks?

13.8 Conclusion

Email and IM are rapidly replacing face-to-face and telephone conversations as the predominant means through which routine workplace communication takes place. As the emerging generations of employees who grew up with email and IM having as part of their world continue to move into senior management, the final barrier to adopting it by the entire workforce, the hesitance to adopt unfamiliar technology, will have been rendered moot.

With the combination of large-scale adoption and immature security, however, email and IM have become popular attack vectors for spammers and phishers. In the manner of the social engineer discussed in Chapter 12, some phishers are now sophisticated enough to be able to gather information unique to an individual in their email campaigns. Through some diligent but not difficult research (such as public records searches and leveraging purchased stolen personal information) a scam artist is able to generate a mosaic of the intended victim to such a degree of perceived authenticity that the target may be lulled into a false sense of security and as such provide the desired information on the spur of the moment. Attacks may come in the "breadth" model, exemplified by the generic email likely sent to millions of recipients all the way down to where a single person is exploited using a "depth" of specific and personal information. A combination of employee education and technology serves an organization best in defending against email- and IM-based attacks.

13.9 Questions for Discussion

Look once again at the phishing email in Figure 13.2. Do you see any other problems with the email that would identify it as a phishing attempt?

Think about your job or a job you are likely to have. What do emails making legitimate requests for proprietary or protected information look like?

- Aside from those obviously legitimate emails, what would an email that would be likely to trick you or someone else in your position to reveal sensitive information need to look like?
- Have you ever had a legitimate email or other request "raise a red flag," and cause you to call to very its veracity? What was it about the request that caused you to do so?

Does your organization have a clear policy on email and IM usage? Are there any types of information that you are not allowed to disseminate over email or IM? Are there any types of information that you *are* allowed to disseminate that should not be communicated over email or IM?

Chapter 14 Network Administration

Chapter Objectives

This chapter will discuss:
- The role of an organization's network administrator from the perspective of managing user access,
- High-level issues influencing how a network administrator ensures security, and
- How network administration fits into the organization's business processes.

14.1 The Network Administrator's Role

In an organization, all the written policies and statements of senior management are worthless unless the people in charge of implementing them do not follow their direction. As was discussed in Chapter 12, a social engineer might be able to convince a network administrator to grant them access by pretending to be someone in dire need of access but who cannot get on the network. The administrator is then convinced to provide a temporary logon, which is all the attacker needs to strike. The following subsections will discuss several aspects of administering user access.

14.1.1 Usernames

This is far more involved than simply determining if the protocol for the organization's email addresses will be "first.last" or "firstinitial.last". Barman (2002) notes several considerations for usernames.

- Handling dormant usernames- If a person has not technically left an organization or is somehow still entitled to have an account with an organization even though they have for all intents and purposes moved on (a very common thing in U.S. colleges and universities), their accounts may go without being used for long periods of time. Should one of those accounts suddenly "come back to life" and begin accessing all sorts of system administrator parts of the network, this should be noted and investigated, especially if the user is an adjunct professor in, for example, the English department.

- Procedures when an employee leaves the organization- As was discussed in the chapter on Initial Employee Communication, an employee should agree to go through a "check out" procedure before they leave. Part of that procedure should be to ensure the IT department has deactivated the separated employee's user accounts.
- Removing default user accounts- In the stories of the "phone phreaking" days, telephone company technicians would leave the default usernames and passwords, such as "field" and "manager" on their systems. This would allow enterprising hackers to access the systems once they obtained the default logon information from the equipment's technical manuals.
- Handling anonymous users- Organizations should be extremely hesitant to allow any type of anonymous access to its networks.
- Assigning all users a pre-configured "role"- A major way to help maintain network security is to define the various roles one may have in an organization and only allow users to be assigned to a role or roles. Exceptions to this practice should be kept to a minimum, as they become extremely difficult to manage.

14.1.2 Passwords

Barman (ibid) continues his analysis of managing user access by arguing that password management may be divided into two parts: what constitutes a valid password and how passwords are to be stored.

In defining a valid password, the long-running conflict between users and network administrators come to bear. Users complain about being required to have a password such as "1Lov#$pR1nger" which must be changed every three months and may not be repeated for several months or years. As discussed elsewhere, brute force methods such as "dictionary attacks," which go through every word in a dictionary, or those which try as many possible letter, number and special character combinations, simply don't work if the password is no less than eight characters, must contain at least one number, at least one special character, and at least one lower- and upper-case letter.

In deciding how to properly store passwords, network administrators realize that it is absolutely essential to keep the organization's passwords out of an outsider's control. Passwords should always be stored in a file that is not easily readable from the outside by being encrypted.

14.2 The Key Business Process Issue Influencing a Network Administrator

In the world of the network administrator, there is a never-ending struggle between those in the offices who complain about the delays and burdens placed on them by security requirements and senior management and the network administrators who see the requirements as a means to ensure security and comply with various regulatory requirements.

All the benefits of having added global connectivity, the business people argue, mean nothing if the system works too slowly to be of any use. Yes, the managers and network administrators argue, but at least we won't go to jail. The balance is a complicated risk management calculation. To guarantee as close to 100% security as possible would mean restricting activity to meaningless levels in many cases. Allowing the business processes to occur in as close to real time as possible, however, would be just as bad on the other side. Each organization, therefore, must decide how risk averse they are and implement policies based on those calculations.

14.3 Network Administrators are Key Players in an Organization's Business Processes

A network administrator influences an organization's business processes. First, they have substantial control over the rights and permissions a user has by assigning roles to the employee if a policy defining the roles they would assume does not exist. This could impact their ability to research information on the organization's network, which poses another risk management calculation: does the potential cost of the employee abusing their privilege outweigh the benefit of their being able to access additional information at their discretion?

Second, the network administrator helps control remote access for employees as well as access for members of the extended enterprise. If the IT department is unable to allow remote users to access the functionalities they require from their home or even from a "foreign" computer at an Internet café, productivity could be reduced substantially. In addition, roles and permissions for those in the extended enterprise, especially customers and suppliers who need to be able to access sales and due-in data, for example, must be developed.

Ultimately, network administrators have a much more difficult job than simply assigning a user a login and password and providing the password back to the user when they forget it; they have substantial input into how well an organization is able to execute its business processes.

14.4 Applying the Balanced Scorecard to the Management Aspects of Network Administration

The goals and their measures in establishing a reference Network Administrator balanced scorecard are:

Goal: Ensure the organization's usernames are properly managed.

- For how long must a username remain dormant before it is deleted or made inactive? What is the percentage of accounts that have reached dormancy that have been acted upon within 24 hours (if none have become dormant, the answer is 100% acted upon).
- Are all employees leaving the organization required to ensure their IT accounts are removed? What percentage of employee accounts are removed within 24 hours after they leave the organization?
- What percentage of default user accounts have been removed, changed or protected in some way?
- How many anonymous users have been allowed to access the organization's networks in the last reporting period?
- What percentage of users are granted privileges based on predefined roles? How many instances of special privileges exist?

Goal: Ensure the organization's passwords are properly managed.

- On a scale of 1-10, what is the "strength" of the required password convention for the organization?
- How often must passwords be changed?
- How long must pass before a password may be re-used?
- What percentage of passwords are stored in encrypted form?

14.5 Conclusion

Network administrators are not simply workers who create user accounts and reset forgotten passwords; they are a critical part of an organization's business process execution. As discussed in Chapter 7, security is critical in ensuring compliance with laws such as Sarbanes-Oxley and as discussed throughout the book proprietary or other sensitive information may be at risk if security is insufficiently tight. On the other hand, the organization must be able to execute its business processes. Network administrators and senior management must work together to determine the proper balance between security and permissiveness.

14.6 Questions for Discussion

What is the protocol for your passwords at your job? How often are you required to change it?

Has the security regime for your network ever delayed your completing your work? Did you complain? Was the security requirement lessened?

For how long have you been able to use the email or access the network of an organization you are no longer with?

Chapter 15 Network Monitoring

Chapter Objectives

This chapter will discuss:
- Intrusion Detection Systems, which include:
- Inspectors,
- Honeypots/Honeywebs, and
- Auditors.

15.1 Monitoring the Network

With the amount of automated and human-generated attacks from around the Internet growing every day, the need to have an automated tool to evaluate what is and is not a threat worth reporting must be addressed. Intrusion Detection Systems (IDS) are the tool to detect, evaluate and block (or audit) the attacks. There are three main types of IDSs:

- Inspectors,
- Decoys, and
- Auditors

15.1.1 Inspectors

The inspector is the most common type of IDS, according to Strebe (2004), and are usually embedded within a firewall. They look for the following indicators of inappropriate use:

- Suspicious network traffic, such as port scans or connections to disallowed ports,
- "Telltales" of known attacks (such as worms or viruses),
- Spikes in resource utilization at unusual times, and
- File activity, such as creating new files, modifying system files or changing user accounts or security settings.

These occurrences are monitored and an audit trail is created for later inspection. Because an IDS relies on its catalog of known attacks, one that is unknown to it will not be detected and as such will not activate the report. Human inspection, therefore, is required as a supplement to the automated work and IDS is able to complete.

15.1.2 Decoys

Decoy IDSs, also known as *honeypots*, are built for the specific purpose of monitoring malicious activity. They "operate by mimicking the expressive behavior of a target system, except instead of providing an intrusion vector for the attacker, they alarm on any use at all. Decoys look just like a real target that hasn't been properly secured." (Strebe, 2004) A honeypot has been defined by the founder of the Honeynet Project as "a security resource whose value lies in being probed, attacked or compromised." (Chuvakin, 2003) The real value comes in the wealth of *by definition* malicious traffic information that is captured and available for analysis.

15.1.3 Auditors

As the name suggests, auditors create audit logs of what everyday users do in their jobs. This audit trail is available for analysis should the need arise. Some operating systems have built-in audit capabilities that can keep track of such things as password changes, spyware installation, changes to system files, etc. Some of the higher-end IDSs will also have the ability to inspect its logs for the telltale signs of an intrusion attempt. If, for example, the password for an admin's account is changed, a "red flag" will go up and a report will be issued to the administrator. (Strebe, 2004)

15.2 IDS' Relevance to the Enterprise

A key factor IDSs bring to the organization is that they allow what they have been programmed to consider to be normal network activity to pass through without note, but will at the very least detect and either passively audit the suspect activity or will actively alert the network administrator to the activity.

The true test comes in configuring the IDS, making sure it reports the correct amount of threats to the network administrators. Should there be such a huge volume of audit logs to be reviewed that it is impossible to do so the real value of the process is lost. As mentioned in the previous chapter, the normal business processes of the organization must be executed in order for it to stay in business or to be effective in its public sector mission.

15.3 Applying the Balanced Scorecard to the Management Aspects of Network Administration

The goals and their measures in establishing a reference Network Monitoring balanced scorecard are:

Goal: Ensure the organization's networks are properly monitored.

- What are our requirements for an IDS? Out of 100%, how do network administrators and senior managers feel the current IDS setup is satisfactory?
- How often are we attacked?
    - By whom are we attacked?
    - What do they "go after" when they attack?
- How long ago did we last update our IDS patterns?
- When an alarm or "red flag" is triggered, what is the average response time?
- When unauthorized access is found to be taking place, how long does it take from when they initially log in until they are locked out?
- When was the last time our audit logs were inspected by humans?

15.4 Conclusion

While this chapter is very brief in order to provide the reader with a high-level introduction to the topic, the importance of high quality intrusion detection cannot be overemphasized. While for some organizations a passive inspector may be enough, for others a full-fledged audit capability may be required. For those organizations wishing to gain a better understanding of how they are attacked, undertaking the construction and maintenance of a honeypot could be a good decision.

15.5 Questions for Discussion

How does your organization currently handle intrusion detection? How often are the logs inspected?

Have you ever had to respond to an incident detected by an intrusion detection system?

How well is your IDS calibrated, meaning how much of the normal stuff gets filtered out, leaving only those incidents that should be investigated left?

Chapter 16 Executive Communication

Chapter Objectives

This chapter will discuss:
- The importance of visible executive support for security initiatives,
- Ronald Coase's theory of Transaction Cost Economics,
- Harvey Leibenstein's theory of X-Inefficiency,
- Mari Sako's theory of Trust, and
- The application of these theories to an organization's security.

16.1 Executive Communication is Crucial in Shaping Employee Behavior

While the communication an employee internalizes most comes from their direct supervisor, as will be discussed in the following chapter on training, executive communication plays a major role in establishing an organization's priorities. This does not mean, however, that a single email or memo from the owner or CEO will be enough to change frontline employee behavior to conform to the required standards to protect network security. Top-down direction is necessary but not usually sufficient to ensure compliance with any direction. Because workers perform in accordance with how they are evaluated and rewarded, it is important to not only publish statements mandating that certain actions be taken but that the people in charge of implementing the processes have their evaluation and pay criteria based on fulfilling the mission as newly defined. The areas of responsibility can be thought of in the following manner:

First, the business processes of the organization and the responsibility for executing those processes should be assigned from the most senior levels of the organization to the line employees actually doing the work. As discussed in Chapter 10, the processes are comprised of *people* who belong to *organizational units* performing *functions* as part of a *business process*. At the executive level, parties should be put in charge of implementing business processes and should be, whenever possible, in charge of the functions performed in support of their process. When it is not possible for one person to be in charge of the entire business process, they should be required to coordinate as often as necessary with those responsible for the functions. In addition, overlaps between processes (functions that support more than one business process) should be identified and those responsible for each process should also coordinate to ensure all business processes are able to be implemented satisfactorily.

Second, an Executive Committee comprised of the senior executives in charge of business processes should be formed and should meet regularly (monthly is a good start and can be adjusted as necessary) to discuss security-related issues. As issues are identified either by executives or by others in the organization a process for tracking the issues to resolution should be implemented. The issues should be evaluated according to their difficulty, time estimated to complete, policy decisions or waivers that must be obtained, and "downstream" processes or decisions impacted by the decision. If possible, a preferred solution should be suggested. The first priority, however, is that the issue be stated clearly and concisely but completely. A single person should be in charge of ensuring the issue is resolved and status should be reported regularly. A common policy is to require that overdue or problem issues be briefed to the Executive Committee when required.

Third, sub-committees and working groups should be assigned to implement the business decisions made by the Executive Committee and to determine how the directives should ultimately manifest in practice. In the U.S. public sector, this is analogous to what happens with a law. The law, which is a high-level policy decision, is passed by the legislative branch and signed by the President. After the law is enacted, however, the executive branch agency responsible for overseeing the law's enforcement must draft regulations which must be followed in order to be in compliance with the law.

Now that the business processes, senior-level committees and working-level committees have been discussed, it is important for the theoretical underpinnings of an organization's actions to be addressed. Because an organization's profitability or effectiveness is tied to its ability to perform its business processes efficiently, Transaction Cost Economics is mentioned. Because many transactions are implemented either entirely or in part by humans X-inefficiency is mentioned. Finally, because the safeguards required to ensure security is being properly maintained are based on the trust established among organizations, work from the Trust literature is included.

16.2 Ronald Coase's Transaction Cost Economics

IT has led to a significant decrease in the cost of executing transactions within an institution, but with that benefit has come the complication of ensuring that network security is maintained as well as needing to define the role humans play in protecting information as they execute their transactions.

16.2.1 Transaction Costs: Make or Buy?

Economist Ronald Coase developed the theory of Transaction Cost Economics to describe the environment in which organizations make what was then (1939) known as the "make or buy" decision. Now, of course, the decision could include whether to physically make a good or to have an office in another part of the country or world to perform a function. Regardless, the question is a relevant one: should we perform the function ourselves at this facility (make), or should we have someone else do it at another location (buy)? Earlier in the book, the role of security as it relates to business processes throughout the extended enterprise was discussed, and it is a critical question. Economist Harvey Leibenstein (in Acheson, 1994) argued that "perhaps the most important concept in institutional economics is that of transaction costs." Simon (in Leibenstein, 1987) delineated "procedural rationality" and "substantive rationality", in that substantive rationality is agnostic as the way a firm achieves maximization. Rather, it is concerned only with the result of the process, assumed to be maximized output or profit. Procedural rationality, however, deals with the methods used inside the firm to approach maximization. Leibenstein (in Acheson, 1994) lists three factors that increase transaction costs:

- *Opportunism*: This involves acting in one's own interests in mind as well as "guile", which could be lying or withholding information, for example. When one is secure in the belief that their workers will not betray the organization, monitoring costs (a part of the total cost of a transaction) are lessened and individual workers are given more flexibility to perform their job as they see fit. When strict procedures are in place, if they are not automatically monitored, they maximize safety while increasing cost.

- *Frequency*: The more transactions that take place, the better each actor is able to make their processes efficient, but it also means that a worker's guard might be let down because of the routine nature of an effective social engineer's approach to them, as was discussed in Chapter 12.
- *Asset Specificity*: When there is a "gatekeeper" or a definite person or type of person (such as a customer service representative) through which one must go to receive access or information, there is also the danger that the person in the position of trust could take advantage of the situation or could be compromised (blackmailed) into breaking the rules in order to pay off a debt or avoid embarrassing information being made public. As mentioned elsewhere in the book, and as practiced in governments and in some private sector companies, background investigations to determine the amount of trust an organization should give an employee is a good idea.

16.2.2 Transaction Cost Economics and its Relationship with Neoclassical Economics

The critical difference between the economists discussed in this chapter and the neoclassical school is that the neoclassical school leaves no room for transaction costs, information costs, and the role of human involvement in an organization's business processes. North (1990) argues the neoclassical model is incapable of addressing the relevant issues, in that:

> "The theory is based on the fundamental assumption of scarcity and hence competition; its harmonious implications come from its assumptions about a frictionless exchange process in which property rights are perfectly and costlessly specified and information is likewise costless to acquire. Although the scarcity and hence competition assumption has been robust and has provided the key underpinnings of neoclassical theory, the other assumptions have not survived nearly so well."

Wetty and Becerra-Fernandez (2001) note that trust is a crucial element in reducing transaction costs and assert that savings may be derived through each of the following generators of transaction costs:

- Search costs- The cost of finding the information or party required to perform a business process,
- Information costs- The cost of generating or obtaining the information itself,
- Bargaining costs- The cost of negotiating the requirements of a transaction,
- Decision costs- The cost incurred from determining the proper course of action,
- Policing costs- The cost of observing and monitoring activities for compliance and non-compliance, and
- Enforcement costs- The cost involved of disciplining those who violate security rules, including the costs involved in prosecuting suspected violations of the law.

A major benefit of a reduction in individual discretion is that the search, information, bargaining and decision costs are high at first but are amortized as business processes are executed several, if not thousands or tens of thousands of times. Policing and enforcement costs go up after the process has been implemented, but the standardization of the security procedure should reduce the cost of the individual policing action because of the standardized nature of the processes, and enforcement should also be more clear-cut because of the suggested policy of "anything that is not in accordance with this procedure is not allowed."

Ultimately, transaction costs are a key unit of analysis in determining an organization's operational effectiveness. Not only is it important to determine the processes and the steps involved, but, as will be seen in the next section, the level of effort required to execute business processes effectively must be maintained.

16.3 Leibenstein's Theory of X-Inefficiency

"The main line (economic) theory assumes that firms minimize costs and hence inputs will be used as effectively as possible. Thus, the question of the degree of the effectiveness of the utilization of inputs cannot even be raised as a question within the traditional theory. But is this question unimportant?"—Harvey Leibenstein (1978)

16.3.1 The Individual is the Proper Unit of Analysis

The neoclassical model of economics relies on several assumptions to make its claims. Two of them, that a firm will minimize its costs and will therefore use inputs to maximum efficiency, are the keys to Harvey Leibenstein's critique of the neoclassical model in his theory of "X-inefficiency." In his theory, Leibenstein emphasizes the role of the individual as a part of the organization rather than the organization of the whole as the unit of analysis. In analyzing the present system of organizations, there are countless points at which a human's actions based on their judgment are required, even though every attempt has been made to automate as many decisions as possible. So, while modern IT implementations come closer to conforming with the neoclassical model through automating many human activities, inefficiency still exists because of the need for human inputs.

Leibenstein (1978) argued that in the neoclassical model households or firms are the unit of analysis, which would assume that each employee would be making optimally efficient decisions concerning the organization's business decisions. All relevant information is assumed to be available. The resulting allocation of inputs is thus assumed to be optimal. In the end, competition is seen as the ultimate arbiter of success and survival. Those who choose wisely will enjoy the fruits of success while those who chose poorly will be forced to correct course or be faced with extinction (North, 1990).

Microeconomics assumes away the internal efficiency issue through using a production function in combination with a maximization postulate. At that point, the maximally efficient use of its inputs is a given. (Leibenstein, 1987) Schumpeter (1939, in Perelman, 2001) insisted "[aggregation] keeps the analysis on the surface of things and prevents it from penetrating into the industrial processes below, which are really what matters. It invites a mechanistic and formalistic treatment of a few isolated contour lines and attributes to aggregates a life of their own and a causal significance they do not possess."

In the real world, no-one would argue that perfect information and perfect efficiency exist, but the claim is made that the neoclassical model is the best predictor of future success. Those who come closest to optimality will win and those who do not will lose. North (1990) argues the neoclassical model forces the organizations that will ultimately survive to discover the information necessary to correct or maintain their correct orientation, but contends that, in fact, individuals often take action based on incomplete or erroneous information (see, for example, the discussion on social engineering earlier in the book, in which employees are duped into revealing data or access to unauthorized individuals through subterfuge).

> **Important:** While at the highest levels aggregated data ultimately shows the health of the organization, it is the actions of each individual employee that generate the data points to be aggregated.

16.3.2 Constraining Influences

Throughout Leibenstein's work is the idea of constraining influences. The first constraint focuses on tradition, in that "things have never been done that way before, so it can't be the right way to do things." This issue manifests itself in many instances, but a public sector example serves as a major case in point. The U.S. Department of Defense (DOD) has for several years been attempting to replace their decades-old, custom-coded IT systems with Commercial-off-the-Shelf (COTS) enterprise resource planning (ERP) packages, such as those from SAP and Oracle. As many readers will know, ERP packages from these vendors have applied best business practices and operate best when implemented as designed, with the organization changing its business processes to conform to the packaged software and reserving any custom coding for areas in which it has special requirements or competitive advantage.

In the case of many public sector implementations with which the author has been directly involved at the governance level, the organizations contracting to have the ERP packages implemented have been unwilling to change their internal processes to conform to the requirements of the ERP package, which has forced the lead system integrator to do its best to contort the software to perform as desired. Doing so has led to a crippling level of complexity and rework and has contributed to what, in the author's opinion, is a lack of success in DOD ERP projects.

Leibenstein (1976) elaborates on the impact a superior may have on their workers in his discussion of the "carte-blanche" principal, which notes that when someone has the ability to impose their choice of bureaucratic constraints with impunity, the result will make people less likely to take initiative, in that the onus to overcome when trying to innovate or change standard operating procedure would make a person who would otherwise be willing to try new things unwilling to take on what would amount to two additional tasks: discovering and implementing the new way of doing things on top of convincing the bureaucracy to allow the new process to be implemented. This has important implications in the public sector, in which one may argue the number of bureaucratic hurdles to cross makes civil servants unwilling to innovate.

16.3.3 Inert Areas

In attempting to innovate and adapt to an every-changing environment, an organization must be able to bring in, digest and leverage information to the greatest extent possible. To wit:

> "One of the firm's most important decision areas lies in recognizing signals from the environment. First, the firm must distinguish between routine signals, and those which indicate changes in the environmental situation, or changes in potential technology. Second, problems may result from the evaluation and channeling of signals from those who receive them from the external world to those within the firm who can best evaluate them and make decisions on that basis. A large number of nonoptimal states persist in this area. Those who receive important signals may not be in a position to process them and send through the appropriate channels. This is an area where a possible arbitrary use of power within the firm as well as arbitrary bureaucratic procedures may prevent of fail to motivate those who have useful information about the environment to channel such information to the appropriate decision-makers." (Leibenstein, 1976)

It is the ability to bring in, assess and process the information available that contributes to the optimization of the production process and leaves open the possibility that what Leibenstein (1987) refers to as "inert areas" will result in suboptimal production implementations. The neoclassical model assumes decisions are made at the organization level, but when humans are required to determine how to accomplish a task, such as whether to release information to a caller or follow security procedures "to the letter" on their own. In doing so, Leibenstein notes that people are subject to a certain level of inertia in their decision-making process (1978), and that when within the bounds of their inert area they will default to a familiar decision. A person typically settles into an inert area through discerning what are known and allowable "effort positions," and assigns a level of utility derived from that position. When a person achieves equilibrium between effort and reward that person adopts that position as their personal optimal effort position (rarely at maximum effort). This "position preference" leads people to avoid looking outside their inert area because the monetary and emotional cost involved in finding a new effort position is more than they are willing to expend. The more entrenched this position preference the more likely attempts will be made to avoid deriving a new one. (Leibenstein, 1976). The role of calculated (maximizing) and uncalculated (non-maximizing) decisions is important.

16.3.4 Principals and Agents

When a person is taken outside the boundaries of their inert area they begin to look for new solutions. (Leibenstein, 1987) "In some contexts, it may be especially useful to distinguish two separate components of the inert area theory: (1) the utility cost of moving away from the present position—i.e. 'packing up' costs, so to speak and (2) the utility cost of getting set up and 'settling into' the new position." (ibid, 1978) The relationship between performance and pressure was established by Yerkes and Dodson. The Yerkes-Dodson Law notes that effectiveness increases until a certain level of stress is reached, flattens out for a time and then decreases as stress begins to overwhelm one's ability to perform under the resultant pressure. (1908, in Leibenstein, 1987) The distinction between how a person with a direct financial stake (a principal) and a person who "only works there" (an agent) determines their effort level is very important.

In a typical principal-agent relationship the principal will attempt to compel agents to act in the best interests of the principals. (Wright and Mukherji, 1999) Because principals are seen as having a neutral reaction to risk and agents are argued to have an aversion because of their inability to spread their interests across several jobs (Eisenhardt, 1989 in Wright and Mukherji, 1999), principals will therefore attempt to wrest an effort level closes to maximum efficiency from their agents while the agents will use their superior knowledge to pursue goals that aid them rather than the principal (Donaldson, 1990 in Wright and Mukherji, 1999). Leibenstein (1976) notes that in large organizations the workers are so far removed from the true principals that they often do not have a strong connection to the organization. It becomes very difficult to define "gain" when there is a large amount of distance between principals and agents. "In some ultimate sense we attempt to interpret gain in terms of utility, but this ceases to be a clear notion when the principals are a large group of shareholders or all the citizens of a country." (ibid)

In discussing the efforts of agents versus those of principals it is worth briefly noting two studies addressing their motivations mentioned in the same literature as X-inefficiency. Wrong (1961, in Eisenhardt, 1988) noted that factory workers tend to be more responsive to attitudes than to monetary inducements, while J.P. Shelton (in Leibenstein, 1976) found in a study of a chain of restaurants than those run by franchises were more profitable than those run by owner-operators. An executive in the company concluded that "franchise owners just watch the little things closer; they utilize the cooks and waitresses better: *they reduce waste*." (emphasis added in Leibenstein)

16.3.5 Activity, Pace, Quality and Time

Over the years many have seen the marginally comedic sign "Price, Quality, Speed: Pick Any Two." This bit of folk wisdom captures a concept that has become a business rule of thumb: if one wants an item completed with a certain amount of speed at a certain quality level they must be willing to pay extra. If you want high quality at a good price you must be willing to wait until the producer is able to fit it into its schedule. If the priority is price and speed of delivery, quality must be sacrificed.

In the current economic environment, of course, the sacrifice of one of the three qualities is not possible, at least not to the extent it has been in the past. Tasks must be accomplished and products must be provided at high quality levels, at reasonable prices and on ever-shorter notice. Leibenstein (1978) provided a framework for analyzing how workers act in carrying out their assignments when he identified activities, pace, quality and time as the key elements in evaluating effort.

The activity required of a worker is the most obvious element of what a person must do to accomplish their assignments. The pace one must maintain while doing their job is critical for one's ability to meet the duties of their position as well as allow others to do their job, which is linked to the sequence and duration of activities in the job.

Fritz (1996, in Coe, 1997) argues that an organization will oscillate between effectiveness and efficiency, citing the example of a company aiming to cut costs by reducing the quality of service delivered to customers. In time this diminished quality of service will be felt in the bottom line and the company will increase service quality to make up for the lost revenue. Such vacillation may be avoided by finding an equilibrium of service and cost, but that notion is far easier to theorize than to operationalize. Perelman (2001) notes that procedural systems will tend to develop obstacles to efficiency through "workarounds" and when gaps or obstacles occur there will be some situations when it is impossible for the system to adapt to meet the situation. "It is not only what people do, but also failure to change when appropriate that may be a source of inefficiency. Hence, the decision procedures are bounded by wide inert areas for individuals and groups, this can lead to inadequate responses to circumstances requiring changes." (ibid)

16.4 Mari Sako's Analysis of Trust

As interactions between geographically disparate locations and people has become commonplace, the need to establish a trusting relationship among those participating in a business process across the extended enterprise to ensure network security has become ever more critical over time.

In the case of procurement, for instance, two-thirds of the respondents to a Pricewaterhouse Coopers study (reported in Ward, 2000) said a trusting relationship with their suppliers was essential before they would be willing to do business with them over the internet. In other cases, the buyers, who are no longer required to spend their time manually processing transactions, have been re-deployed to develop ongoing relationships with suppliers through negotiations. This works especially well for companies with very large levels of procurement (IBM, Sun Microsystems, Proctor & Gamble and Whirlpool, for example).

16.4.1 Arms-Length and Obligational Contractual Relationships

When it comes to trust, Sako (1992) provides a useful theoretical framework for addressing trust in her distinction of "Arms-Length" and "Obligational" contractual relations, which have the following characteristics:

Arm's Length Contracutal Relations (ACR) "involve(s) a specific, discrete economic transaction. An explicit contract spells out before trading commences each party's tasks and duties in every conceivable eventuality, as far as human capacity for anticipation allows. If unforeseen contingencies arise, they are settled by resort to some universalistic legal or normative rules. All dealing's are thus conducted at arm's length, to avoid undue familiarity, with neither party controlled by the other." (Sako, 1992) Houston (2001) discusses the use of calculativeness in assessing whether or not a partner will fulfill its commitment as promised. Based on Williamson's (1993) description of "calculative trust", the arguments asserts that given sufficient financial incentive the parties to a transaction will execute the terms faithfully.

Obligational Contractual Relations (OCR) "also involve an economic contract covering the production and trading of goods and services. But it is embedded in more particularistic social relations between trading partners who entertain a sense of mutual trust. Because of this underpinning, transactions take place without prior agreement on all the terms and conditions of the trade.

16.4.2 Dimensions of Trust

In her framework, Sako delineates two dimensions in which the differences between ACR and OCR manifest themselves. Interdependence, the first of Sako's dimensions, refers to a situation in which one party's actions have a direct bearing on the condition of its trading partner, with the timespan for reciprocity being the second. ACR would only require contractual trust, the belief that a trading partner will live up to the letter of a written agreement but no more, and be responsible for any damages of defaulting on its commitments.

For an OCR relationship, there exists goodwill trust, in which one partner would be potentially willing to grant a request for a change in any area (an "open" relationship, according to Leibenstein, 1987) or in only some areas (a "limited" relationship, per Leibenstein [ibid]). When considering the timespan for reciprocity, the distinction between ACR and OCR relationships is no less clear. Because an ACR relationship is focused solel on the timeframe in which an existing contract is in force, there is no consideration of the ability to gain "payback" for any favors past the contracts' expiration. For an OCR relationship, the time to collect on a favor need not occur in the short term. Rather, it may be saved, knowing that the other party will remember and be willing to accommodate. Houston

(2001) used the notion of "empathetic trust", two entities internalizing each other's values, to make the point.

A third type of trust Sako discusses is competence trust. This, as the name implies, is the belief that the trading partner will be able to perform its contractual obligations at an acceptable level of quality. As in interpersonal relations, all the goodwill and effort in the world will not allow someone to do something they are simply incapable of doing. In the professional world, there will be times when an organization will either with full knowledge or through underestimating the difficulty of a proposed task, overpromise on a contract. When those tasked to depend on the contract award winner for the product or service they have promised to deliver do not have faith in the ability of the organization to meet their requirements, or if they feel that the product or service does not meet their needs adequately, then they will find ways to work around or avoid it.

It should be noted that an increase in competence trust might lead to a transition from ACR to OCR. A common technique organizations use with new partners is to grant them a relatively small award and observe how they perform with an eye on future grants. Exemplary performers will gradually earn a greater share of the responsibility or sales, but with the increased income comes the increased burden of having a larger proportion of its income come from the single source. McMaster and Sawkins (1996) discuss the value of trust as, among other things, requiring credible commitment citing North (1993) and as something that can be lost in an instant (Leibenstein, 1987). They also note Arrow's (1973) contention that no transaction is conducted without an element of trust.

16.4.3 Trust's Role in Transaction Cost Economics

While expensive to establish, trusting business relationships save money over time. Analogous to the accounting techniques of amortizing and depreciating investments, the initial cost of developing trust pays dividends in every transaction performed through the mechanism enabled by the relationship. Pressure, as Leibenstein (1976) uses the term, creates the motivation to find a new "best" partner but could also lead to the search for better partners to cease when a certain comfort level has been achieved.

As it relates to network security, an OCR is very difficult to justify because of the sheer magnitude of liability attached to any failure to maintain security. In fact, because of the risk management aspect of the auditing procedures for regulatory compliance, Arms-Length trust is the only way to go.

16.5 Applying the Balanced Scorecard to Executive Communication

The goals and their measures in establishing a reference Executive Communication balanced scorecard are:

Goal: Establish responsibility for business processes.
- Business processes defined completely-
    - o Have the functions to be performed within the business processes been defined?
    - o Have the people/organizations responsible for performing the functions been identified?
    - o Have the IT systems used to implement the functions been identified?
    - o Has the data associated with the business processes been identified as to its origin and level of security?
    - o How long ago were these last validated?
- Executive committees formed-
    - o Are the roles in the committee aligned with the executive's responsibilities to the organization?
    - o Is the process for resolving conflicts between the functional and process leaders established?
    - o How long ago were these last validated?
- Sub-committees formed-
    - o Are subcommittees who are answerable to the senior executives comprised of the correct people?
    - o Do the subcommittees meet regularly? How long ago did they last meet?
    - o Do the subcommittees properly elevate issues they are not able to resolve to the senior executives for decisions?
    - o How long has it taken for each issue assigned to the subcommittees to be resolved?
    - o How long ago was the makeup of these committees last reviewed?

Goal: Establish a baseline for costs and effort levels
- Business process costs determined-
    - o To the extent necessary or possible, have the costs of performing each business process been identified?

- o   Has each cost been assigned to a business process versus a functional stovepipe?
- o   When were these costs and assignments last validated?
- Acceptable effort levels for each function determined-
    - o   For each function to be performed, has an acceptable and measurable effort level been established?
    - o   Are ways of improving the processes being investigated?
    - o   How often are the effort levels and investigations updated?

16.6 Conclusion

Communication at the executive level is a critical element in the overall success of an organization; in order for lower-level managers to know the organization's goals and priorities, senior organization officials must take the time to establish them and communicate them to those charged with realizing them in practice. Three theoretical constructs; Transaction Cost Economics, X-inefficiency, and Sako's discussion on Trust help put the role of communication and employee and inter-organizational collaboration in how effectively an organization implements its business practices in proper perspective.

16.7 Questions for Discussion

In your organization, how are executive-level issues identified and resolved? If you had a question or concern about the business process you support, to whom would the question be addressed? If you don't know, whom would you ask?

Are you part of or aware of standing committees in your organization charged with addressing issues and reporting them to higher-level committees or single executives? How often do they meet? After your committee does its work, do you ever hear of the issue again? Is there consistent follow-through on your suggestions or concerns?

Think of the business process or processes you support.

What do you do during a typical day?
With whom do you communicate?

How do you know the person requesting information from you is entitled to receive it?

Do you have set goals or criteria for what is expected of you on a daily, weekly or monthly basis?

Now remember the discussion of social engineering from Chapter 12.

If you wanted to trick someone in your job to disclose the information to which you have access, what would it take for you to give it to them?

In your experience, what has happened during a routine transaction that "just didn't seem right"? Did you refuse to disclose the information? Did you know the person asking you for the information?

Chapter 17 Information Security Awareness

Chapter Objectives

This chapter will discuss:
- Ensuring employees understand their role in security;
- The elements of information security awareness training;
- Training and its methods of delivery; and
- Change management.

17.1 Ensuring Employees Understand Their Role in Security

Throughout the book, especially in Chapters 12 and 13, the threats posed to an organization through parties attempting to trick employees into disclosing sensitive information were detailed. In Chapter 11, the task of communicating to an employee their responsibilities for protecting information and the range of possible consequences should they be found to have released information to an unauthorized party, especially through negligence.

17.1.1 Social Engineering

In Chapter 12, the "human element" was shown to be a key player in how information is released inappropriately. Leveraging intimate knowledge of human psychology, social engineers are far too often able to exploit our weaknesses to their advantage. As this book's author is an American, the psychological tendencies discussed are those of Americans and may or may not apply to another culture, or may need to be exploited differently in other cultures. Also, it is worth noting, the word *tendencies* is used purposefully, as not all Americans will behave in the same way.

17.2.2 Phishing

In Chapter 13, we covered the role phishing plays in the maturing world of email and instant message communication. This is also a type of social engineering, as the scam artists are attempting to capitalize on: a person's willingness to help others (someone in dire straits) , a person's fear (such as a credit card account being canceled unless specific information is provided to keep it alive) or greed (I'm in another country and need to transfer money out FAST! Give me your bank account information so I can send it to you and you can keep some of it.) These techniques don't work very often, but the fraudsters are becoming more sophisticated, as the case of the personalized credit union emails established. Even something as seemingly innocuous as clicking on a link sent in an email or instant message could risk exposing the user to a virus, spyware or keylogger.

17.2.3 Initial Employee Communication

Informing a new employee of the organization's expectations of them regarding their handling of controlled information is important, as it will set the tone for their work. A properly worded employee agreement stating the organization's policies on handling information provides the employer with "cover" should an employee violate its policies.

17.3 Information Security Awareness' Elements

While an organization has the right to protect itself against unauthorized disclosures, it also has an obligation to provide training to its employees to guide them as to what is approved and appropriate behavior and what is not as it pertains to handling information.

Peltier (2005), argues that learning for security awareness has three key aspects:

- "*Awareness*, which is used to stimulate, motivate, and remind the audience what is expected of them.
- "*Training*, the process that teaches a skill or the use of a required tool.
- "*Education*, the specialized, in-depth schooling required to support the tools or as a career development process."

In developing an information security awareness training regime, the organization's human resources department should work in conjunction with the IT department to ensure that the training adequately addresses the topic area but also conforms to relevant laws and regulations. (Coe, 2003)

Unfortunately, training is not simply a "one size fits all" situation; McCoy and Fowler (2004) note that there are multiple audiences to be addressed when dealing with IT security. An obvious example is that a senior executive would not need to know the procedure one must go through at the operational level to release information. Instead, what the executive would need to know is that they should never instruct someone to release sensitive information unless they are 100% certain the requirement for the information is legitimate.

It is obvious but still worth stating that if an executive requests information from a rank-and-file employee that the junior person will almost certainly provide it without question, and as such the burden falls on the executive to ensure the request is proper. To ensure an audit trail exists, sensitive information should never be disseminated based on a verbal request alone. An email from the requestor should be required, and if a senior person requests information from a junior employee verbally the person providing the information should send a "clarifying" email documenting the data to be delivered and should receive an affirmative response from the requestor. The employee may not "need to know" who will ultimately receive the information, nor the purpose for which it will be used, but they do have the absolute requirement to know that the request is legitimate, which is established with them by an auditable message. Employees should also know who is authorized to make requests and should be comfortable passing requests from those not on the authorized requestor list to their superiors.

17.4 Methods of Delivering Training

The actual ways in which training is delivered have evolved over time to include information technology as the medium. Page (2000) details nine methods now in common use.

17.4.1 Lecture

Lecture is the most traditional training method, and is still used quite often. In this setting, an instructor delivers the content in a classroom or auditorium and the audience either physically present or connected in via video teleconference or a strictly audio teleconference. The lecture format is ideally suited for "overview" training, in which concepts rather than details being the intended "take-away" for the attendees. As many of those reading the book will know, lecture training often consists of showing up, signing in, listening (or pretending to listen) to the lecture and then leaving with no follow-up or test to ascertain what has been retained.

17.4.2 Workshops

Another method using a group setting is the workshop. In a workshop, however the goal is for attendees to participate actively in the learning as opposed to the passive environment of the lecture format. Workshops are usually short in duration, no longer, than an hour, and are held at the participants' worksite. The relatively small number of attendees (generally 20 or fewer) means the lead is able to be a facilitator rather than an instructor, and the topics covered may be tailored to apply to the small group's specific requirements.

17.4.3 Department Meetings

While the term "department" might not apply in every case, organizations usually have distinct divisions of labor, usually by functional area. In this case, the training is delivered or facilitated by the normal meeting leader. Because these meetings involve people who usually work side-by-side, the topics covered may be tailored to the specific needs of the group.

17.4.4 Structured On-the-Job-Training

After or even instead of a lecture training session, on-the-job-training (OJT) is a way to quickly teach a worker how to perform a task. OJT has seven steps (Jacoba, 1995):

1. Show the employee how to perform the task;
2. Explain the key points of the task;
3. Allow the employee to watch as you perform the task;
4. Allow the employee to perform the simple parts of the task under your supervision;
5. Help the employee perform the entire task;
6. Watch the employee as they perform the entire task by themselves; and
7. Allow the employee to perform the task entirely on their own.

This task is very helpful for showing employees how to accomplish specific tasks in isolation ("Type 1 learning") but is worthless when the goal is to help employees apply general concepts to specific situations ("Type 2 learning). Structured OJT teaches employees what to think rather than how to think.

17.4.5 Multimedia Training

Multimedia training takes place on a computer and involves two or more media:

- Text;
- Graphics;
- Animation;
- Audio; and
- Video

This type of training is generally engaging for the user and allows the student to proceed at their own pace.

17.4.6 CD-ROM Training

CD-ROM training is a self-contained training package on a single compact disk (DVD-ROMs are now available- author) which may be consumed by the student at their convenience on their own computer, assuming it has the necessary drives. The storage capabilities on disk media have grown to the point where significant amounts of video and volumes of training manuals may be put on every disk.

17.4.7 Computer-Based Training

Computer-Based Training (CBT) is the umbrella term for all training that takes place on a computer, including CD-ROM and Web-based training. CBT is also referred to as Computer-assisted Instruction (CAI), which "is a computer program coded to display prompts and instructions to a student plus information and interactive exercises on a subject or topic. Moreover, the program is coded to keep track of the student's path and to offer immediate response to the student's input" and would be excellent for policies and procedures training. (Page, 2000)

17.4.8 Web-Based Training

As the name suggest, Web-Based Training (WBT) is distributed over the organization's intranet or via the Web to the student's computer. Because Web access is so widespread, it is easily accessible. The advantages of WBT are:

- It is available cross-platform;
- It is readily available;
- It can be delivered at any time (flexibility);
- As long as the site is available and the student's Web connection is working, the training may be accesses;
- It is convenient, as training may be accomplished at any time;
- Because of the "build it once and use it a thousand times" model, there is significant cost savings; and
- The training is easily updated, as individual binders do not need to have pages replaced.

17.4.9 Computer-Assisted Network Discussion Groups

The nature of the Web enables students to join in a discussion with others from anywhere in the world as long as their system is properly equiped to allow them to access a discussion group. Network discussion groups may be considered in two different ways: asynchronous and synchronous.

Asynchronous groups are what most users would interpret as "discussion groups." These groups are email-based and as such are not occurring in real time, although when the participants become impassioned it is near-real time. Users will typically join a group and follow discussion "threads" that pique their interest. Participation in these groups ranges from occasional "lurking" (simply reading what others have written without posting any messages of their own) to being someone who, it seems, is posting every other message. These groups, when members voluntarily or a moderator ensures the discussion stays on topic, are very useful for sharing information and perspective.

Synchronous groups are becoming more and more popular as the technology to allow for geographically distant users to edit the same document or presentation simultaneously. These products allow for what could be referred to as the "7" meeting, in which one group for whom it is 7 am can meet with another group for whom it is 7 pm without sacrificing much of their ability to interact directly.

Important: Using actual cases from your or other organizations is a suggested way to move the training discussion from the abstract to the real in the minds of the students. It also establishes that, while the perpetrator may not have violated policy or law intentionally, or if they did and were able to go undetected for a period of time, they were eventually found out and dealt with.

17.5 Change Management

In any environment in which there is significant change, there is likely to be resistance. This section will address information security awareness with the assumption that it is not ingrained to the extent it must be in the current regulatory environment and that a significant shift in the mindset of employee attitudes and practices toward information security must be undertaken. Because of the real and significant potential organizational and personal consequences of breakdowns in information security, clear and firm policies must be established, perhaps in the face of active or passive opposition.

Lewin (1952) classified that significant changes come in three stages:

- Unfreezing
- Making the Transition, and
- Refreezing

Iskat and Liebowitz (2003) took Lewin's three phases and formed thirteen principles among them.

17.5.1 Unfreezing

The first principle under unfreezing is *provide your rationale*. Many readers have experienced a policy being handed down "from on high" with no explanation. When this happens, there is no understanding on the employee's part and often means the policy will not be "internalized" and seen as legitimate. When the reasons behind the policy and how it will contribute to the good of the organization are described to the employees, however, they will know that management feels it is important for workers to know why decisions have been made, even if they were not given any input into forming the policy. This is a much more respectful posture to take than to simply inform the employees of a decision as if it is a royal edict.

The second principle is to *be empathetic*. While the decision will have been made in order to forward the goals of the organization, when employees are impacted there could very well be significant levels of stress involved. In addition to acknowledging that major change is ongoing, management should do what it can to mitigate any negative impacts.

Third, management should *communicate clearly* with the workforce. Whether you call it the "rumor mill," the "grapevine" or something else, the more people are forced to guess about what is or will be happening and who it will impact the wilder the speculation will become. As much detail as possible should be shared with the employees, including the steps to be taken in moving from the "as-is" to the "to-be" environments. By doing this, the employees understand the process and will be more able to deal with it while getting on with their job.

17.5.2 Making the Transition

As employees are expected to begin conforming to the new regime of network security policies and procedures, they will perhaps be required to read and acknowledge they understand and will abide by the new requirements and that they are aware of the possible consequences of violating the policies. As mentioned earlier in the book, Leibenstein discusses the concept of an employee's *effort position*, in that they will have found a pace, level of quality, and time to complete the activities required of them in their jobs. For those workers in positions which require knowing when and when not to provide sensitive information the new situation could be a major subject of stress. The following principles are intended to reduce the anxiety as much as possible.

First, the organization should be sure to *explain the benefits* of the change. One benefit for the employee would be that the ways in which they are expected to behave and the procedures they are expected to follow, while perhaps more burdensome than before, will actually serve the employee well because what is allowed and what is not is now defined clearly. In addition, each employee should know that the changes are being made for a specific reason, such as improving business processes or protecting the organization and the individual employee from running afoul of laws or regulations.

Second, management should *identify a champion* who will serve as the "face" of the initiative. The best person for the job is a respected manager who takes on the role voluntarily. Other people who may not be members of management but whose opinion is considered highly by other employees should also be asked to help advocate the changes after they understand the rationale behind the initiative.

Third, wherever possible those organizing the initiative should *obtain participative input*. While some line employees don't have an interest in how their job impacts the rest of the organization they will know how to best do their own jobs and would likely be able to suggest ways of improving the processes they perform that would fit into the new regime.

> **Important:** It is extremely disconfirming and counterproductive to ask an employee for input and then not consider it or to consider it but not accept the recommendation without providing the employee some sort of explanation and an expression of thanks for their efforts. Often, the input will have been generated during time in which they would otherwise have been doing their regular job or enjoying time off. To an employee, being asked to go above and beyond their normal call of duty only to have what they gave as input disappear into what they see as a black hole is worse than having never asked for the input in the first place.

Fourth, one should always *be aware of the timing* of the initiative. When possible, the busiest seasons should be avoided, such as a retailer avoiding trying a major change during the holiday shopping season in the U.S. or attempting to hold mandatory workshops in August in Germany. Both of the above are horrible ideas.

Fifth, wherever possible the organization should promise to *maintain job security*. This typically applies when business process reengineering is taking place, but it also applies here. Ultimately, the employees should know that the new regime is *not* an effort to trim the workforce (unless, of course, it is) but is aimed toward strengthening the organization's security regime.

Sixth, employees with enhanced security expectations should know they will be *provided with training* to enable them to meet their new burdens. Always emphasize to the workers that training makes them more valuable to the organization, which means their short-term anxiety will result in more long-term job security.

Finally, change should *proceed at a manageable pace*. Employees enthused by a change can have their good will crushed under the weight of a "forced march." As has been noted several times throughout the book, most people hate change, especially when it comes to changes affecting how they support their families. As calm and measured a pace as possible should be taken.

17.5.3 Refreezing

After the change process is complete, the final step is to make the "to-be" the new "as-is." The first step to do this is to *indicate top management's support* that the process is complete and begins behaving in ways consistent with the new stated policies. Because workers look to see what managers do rather than what they say, they will ignore the new policies if they see their managers behaving the old way.

> **Important:** A key consideration in ensuring managers will abide by the new status quo comes in adjusting their compensation schemes to reflect the new direction. Because most people are motivated to maximize their financial rewards, if line employees, managers and executives are still paid based on the standards of the old system, it will be extremely difficult to convince them to change the way they do their jobs.

Next, the organization should *publicize successes and make mid-course corrections where needed*. Not everything will go as well as hoped, but there will certainly be some bright spots. These encouraging signs should be emphasized in meetings, emails and other communication. Just as important, if not more so, is to recognize when something is not going to succeed as originally planned. In some cases, pride must be swallowed and changes made, not as a knee-jerk reaction but rather as a well-considered analysis of alternatives.

Finally, the organization should *provide employee services*. Employee assistance programs can help arrest problems before they develop into distractions. Anxiety, as mentioned earlier, is a common outcome of major change. Counseling, mentoring and additional training are all steps that could be taken to help employees cope with their new work environment.

17.6 Applying the Balanced Scorecard to Training

The goals and their measures in establishing a reference Information Security Awareness balanced scorecard are:

Goal: Ensure the organization understands Information Security Awareness.
- Awareness is understood-
    - o Has management considered the proper message and medium for ensuring awareness?
    - o Has management worked with human resources to understand which employees require specific reminders based on their position within the organization?
    - o How long ago was the last update?
- Training and education are undertaken-
    - o Has the proper method or mix of methods for training and education been determined?
    - o If training must be undertaken over the Web or over the organization's Intranet, does current IT policy allow for the applications needed to perform the training to be run on the network?
    - o Is there a well-organized and publicized discussion group for employees to join and share ideas?
    - o As for discussion groups, are persons outside of the organization allowed to participate?
    - o If outsiders are allowed to participate, are certain lines of discussion off limits?
    - o Should there be discussion groups for those within the organization only in addition to discussion groups in which outsiders are included?
    - o How long ago was the "mix" of training methods last evaluated and updated?

Goal: Ensure change management is performed well.
- The status quo ("as-is") is unfrozen-
    - o Has management provided a clear rationale to the workforce as to why the change is being made?

- o Is management demonstrating that the organization understands and empathizes with the employees' stress in going through change?
- o Is management communicating clearly as to what is taking place and what is going to be taking place in the future?
- o What is the percentage of employees agreeing that management is communicating company policy and its rationale effectively?
- The transition is made-
  - o Has management explained the benefits of the change?
  - o Has management identified a champion or champions of sufficient stature to give the change regime legitimacy?
  - o Has management obtained participant input and has that input been considered and the participants provided with feedback regardless of whether their input was ultimately adopted as policy?
  - o Has management considered carefully the impact of the timing of the transition on normal operations?
  - o If possible, has the organization assured its employees that job security is being maintained?
  - o Do employees understand they will be provided with training to prepare themselves for the new situation?
  - o Will the change proceed at a sufficiently gradual pace to minimize employee anxiety to the greatest extent possible?
  - o What percentage of employees agree that all of these questions have been answered satisfactorily?
- The new regime ("to-be") is established-
  - o Has management identified that the change process has concluded and that the new status quo has been established?
  - o Have successes been emphasized and celebrated?
  - o Have mid-course corrections been made where needed?
  - o Has management provided employee services to aid those employees who required extra mentoring or counseling during the change process?
  - o What percentage of employees agree that all of these questions have been answered satisfactorily?

17.7 Conclusion

In the current operating environment, organizations are at significant risk of severe consequences should they release sensitive or controlled information improperly. Unfortunately, absolute security cannot be guaranteed, as workers would be unable to do their jobs because of how long it would take to verify everything needed to get as close to 100% secure as possible. What an organization can do to put itself and its employees in the best position to protect this information is to enact a strong training regime and change management process to bring the organization to where it needs to be. A firm but empathetic tone is the recommended approach, as employees who are overly worried about their jobs are apt to make mistakes, refuse to release information when it is proper to do so, or quit. Instead, the organization should do its utmost to ensure its employees are trained and empowered with the knowledge they need to do their job well.

17.8 Sample Questionnaire

Kim (2005) used the following questionnaire to ascertain how aware employees were of their computer security situation (Note: Edits have been made by the author):

Demographic Information Section

Q1: Are you working full time? Yes □ No □
Q2: Are you: Male □ Female □
Q3: Your age: 10-20 □ 21-30 □ 31-40 □ 41-50 □ 51-65 □
Q4: What is your job title? Please describe your job briefly:

Information Security Awareness Section
Q5: Have you attended any information security workshops or training sessions? Yes □ No □
Q6: Have you ever lost data or files you had previously saved on your computer? Yes □ No □
Q7: If you responded "Yes" on Q6, what was the reason for the loss? Virus □ Computer malfunction □ Other reasons □ Don't know □
Q8: Do you use an anti-virus program on your computer? Yes □ No □ Don't understand the question □
Q9: If you responded "Yes" on Q8, how often do you update your anti-virus program? Never updated □ Automatic update □ Once a week □

Once every two weeks □ Once a month □ Do not know when it is updated □

Q10: Do you use a personal firewall on your computer? Yes □ No □
Don't understand the question □ N/A □

Q11: How often do you check for updates to your Windows operating
system? Never □ Automatic updates □ Once a week □ Once every two
weeks □ Once a month □ Do not know when it was last updated □

Q12: If you update your Windows operating system, how do know if a
new update is available? By email □ Auto-update □ Someone tells me an
update is available □ Regular manual checks □ Other □ (please specify)

Q13: Do you back up any of your data files? Yes □ No □

Q14: How do you remember your user IDs and passwords? Use one
password for all access needs □ Memorize all of them □ Other □ (Please
describe briefly)

Q15: Do you use a spyware detector? Yes □ No □ Don't understand
the question □ N/A □

Q16: Do you think P2P file sharing may cause serious damage to your
computer? Yes □ No □ Don't know □

Q17: Do you know what "phishing" is? Yes □ No □

Q18: If you responded "Yes" to Q17, have you even been "phished"?
Yes □ No □ Don't know □ N/A □

17.9 Questions for Discussion

In the questionnaire directly above, are there any additional questions you would ask an employee about their technology-based security?

Have you been trained on the procedure to follow to authenticate
that a requestor is entitled to the information they want to obtain?

Have you ever been trained on how to detect if you are being
"worked" by a social engineer or phisher? If not, what would be a
sample scenario in which a person would seem to sound legitimate
but would in fact be a scam artist?

While it may be optimal to have employees know all the information requested in the questionnaire above, is it absolutely necessary? Would the fact that the employee needs to be aware of that
information signal something to you about the procedure the organization is using?

The tendencies able to be exploited by social engineers discussed in this book are American-centric. If you have knowledge of other cultures, which tendencies are the same or at least similar to those in American culture? Based on the other culture with which you are familiar, how would you go about a social engineering mission? What are the aspects of that culture that would leave it vulnerable to a social engineering attack?

What have been your experiences with change in your career? Has the message from management been consistent from beginning to end?

How well has management performed with regard to acknowledging employee participation?

During periods of significant change in your career, what was your level of anxiety about the change? Did you continue to worry about your job security even when it was explicitly stated that your position was not in jeopardy? How would your memory of your feeling guide your conduct when you are the management representative communicating with employees?

Chapter 18 Synthesis and Conclusion

Chapter Objectives

This chapter will discuss:
- The current state of an organization's operational environment,
- The transition to service oriented architectures, and
- The utility of a well-developed enterprise architecture.

18.1 The Current State of an Organization's Operational Environment

In the past few decades, organizations' operating environments have changed dramatically. For a significant period of time, computers in an office were simply typewriters able to store documents for future retrieval. Now, the sheer processing power of the common desktop or laptop computer far outpaces what was available only a short time ago. Now that virtually everyone has a computer of some type, and now that instantaneous communication around the world is required of many jobs, the role of network security is even more critical.

18.1.1 An International Business Scenario

Kaplan and Norton (2006), the balanced scorecard pioneers from Chapter 7, discuss how "advantage today is derived less from the management of physical and financial assets and more from how well companies align such intangible assets as knowledge workers, R&D, and IT to the demands of their customers. (Also), the opportunities and challenges that globalization affords are forcing companies to revisit many assumptions about the control and management of both their physical and their intangible assets."

A perhaps typical flow of materiel and information in the modern era is shown in Figure 18.1.

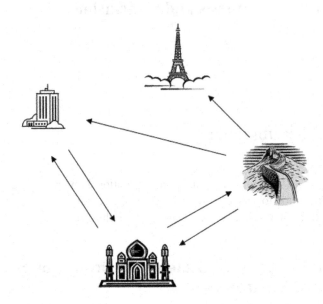

Figure 18.1 Information and Materiel Flow in an International Business Scenario

In this example, several countries are involved: the United States, France, China and India. Each country has sufficient capabilities to easily accomplish any part of this scenario, but assuming for the sake of discussion that:

- The product is designed as well as sold in the United States,
- The product is sold in France,
- The product is manufactured in China, and
- The product's English language customer service is performed in India and feedback and design improvement suggestions are part of the service provided to the American company.

For the American company, there are several considerations:

What is the relative cost of the transaction when so much functionality is distributed around the world?

Referring back to Chapter 16, the arguments of Coase, Leibenstein and Sako apply here. Coase, whose major area of discussion was Transaction Cost Economics, found that organizations would make the decision to "make or buy" based on economic rationality. When the seminal piece was written, the decision to be made was whether or not to make the product internally or to hire an outside but nearby company to do it. With the astounding connectivity afforded by global IT connectivity, however, the decision may now be expanded to include countries half a world away.

The obvious motivation for outsourcing the manufacturing to China and the customer service to India is cost. Because American wages are very high comparatively and a substantial portion of India's approximately one billion citizens are technically savvy and speak English there is a profit-driven reason to send the work overseas. For the manufacturing, hiring a Chinese company carries the same rationale: quality work at the most affordable price.

Why would an organization outsource in the first place?

Leibenstein's X-Inefficiency analysis deals with the motivations of individual employees, but may be analogized to organizations. For example, the United States Government decided it would for the most part become managers and select companies and individuals to provide products and services via competitive bids. In this way, companies are motivated to bid at competitive cost levels, to demonstrate a high degree of expertise in the bid process and to perform to a high level after contract award. In addition, the government is granted the flexibility of renewing or not renewing contracts on a yearly basis, and may even terminate contracts "with cause" or "at convenience" with notice.

In the private sector, it is even more straightforward. As discussed above, for U.S. companies, while there has been significant criticism over what has been referred to as the "hollowing out" of the American economy, the simple fact is that it makes more sense economically to have significant parts of its business processes executed outside of the country because the quality of the good or service received in return is of a sufficient quality to justify the decision. Because companies are beholden to investors or owners, they are motivated to make the best business decision in spite of any personal desires to keep jobs and infrastructure capabilities in the U.S.

How does an organization know the quality will be good and that they won't be "ripped off"?

A major concern of any organization when operating internationally is that the companies they have hired to perform will not do so or will simply "take the money and run." Sako's analysis divides trust into two realms: arms-length and relationship-based. When first doing business with almost any partner, it is preferable to first have them perform relatively insignificant work or to have only a few employees doing the work. In this way, the organization limits its exposure to poor quality and fraud. The outside company is given the opportunity to demonstrate its abilities and reliability, and over time as promises are made and kept and timely payment is received the relationship may grow into one based on the relationship rather than necessarily working to make every penny of profit available.

18.1.2 Service Oriented Architecture- The Extended Enterprise's Next Technological Step

In the 1990s, the trend was to install massively integrated but very cumbersome enterprise resource planning (ERP) systems, such as those offered by SAP and Oracle. For organizations able to do so successfully, which involved re-engineering business processes to conform to the core software capability with the exception of specialized functionality offered by partners, third-party vendors and organic custom development, the benefits were remarkable. For organizations unable to implement ERP, however, they were often forced to revert to legacy systems. What often resulted was what Gulledge (2004) refers to as "islands of automation," in that ERP implementations at individual sites were successful but the organization was not able to integrate among sites.

The emerging technology solution being offered is the Service Oriented Architecture (SOA), which leverages technology to allow all authorized users from across the extended enterprise to access data from its "single source of truth." In the past, as shown in Figure 18.2, different sites were forced to interface with each other individually. This is incredibly complex and expensive and fraught with transmission errors.

What an SOA allows an organization to do instead is to identify the system which creates a piece of data as its originator and to point users requiring that data to it through the use of a "registry," which is a listing of which "web services" are available and where they are located. Figure 18.3 shows the new, simplified configuration which includes an SOA technology enabler such as SAP's NetWeaver. (www.sap.com)

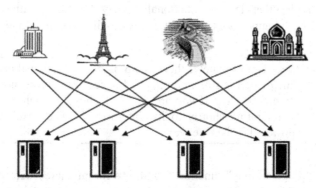

Figure 18.2 The Old Way- Individual Interfaces

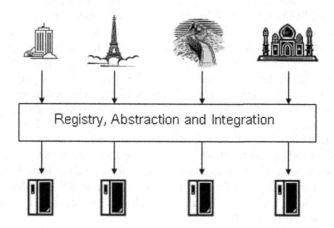

Figure 18.3 The New Way- Service Oriented Architecture

18.2.3 Additional SOA Functionality

The much simpler picture of Figure 18.3 as compared to Figure 18.2 does not mean a less complex operation is occurring. In fact, the need to "orchestrate" the information exchanges among locations is perhaps even more daunting initially. One advantage of an SOA is that the interactions are "loosely coupled," meaning that different functionalities may be added and dropped relatively simply because of the common standards required by the application orchestrating the SOA. This common standard means, for example, that legacy functionality may be fitted with an SOA-compatible "wrapper" that allows the functionality to plug into the SOA.

> **Important:** Unfortunately, there is no single "SOA" at this point. Rather, the market is still emerging and is becoming more and more competitive each day. If you are an "SAP shop," though, you will likely be migrating shortly to its Enterprise Services Architecture (ESA), powered by NetWeaver.

This "plug and play" functionality allows for an unprecedented level of choice on the part of the organization. While in the model presented in Figure 18.2, if a business process was to be changed an entirely new interface would need to be built, tested and activated. Because the very premise of an SOA is to allow for loose coupling, however, already-created functionality may be exchanged with relative ease (but not "easily" yet). Figure 18.4 shows an as-is process and a small function repository to the right. Figure 18.5 shows the same process will all possible options displayed. ARIS, the tool used to compose this model, displays "out of scope" (unused) objects in white. The circled "x", referred to as an *Exclusive Or* or XOR, means only one of the three options on the line below may be used at any given time. In this example, function 2(b) is used in the current process. If the requirements for the process were to change, one of the other two functions may be used to meet the new requirement (two ways in which changes could come about would be through a shift in compliance mandates or through a desire to generate different data outputs for reporting purposes.) Figure 18.6 shows the reconfigured process. (Svensson and Frye, 2005)

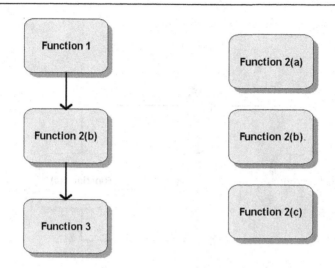

Figure 18.4 The As-Is Process

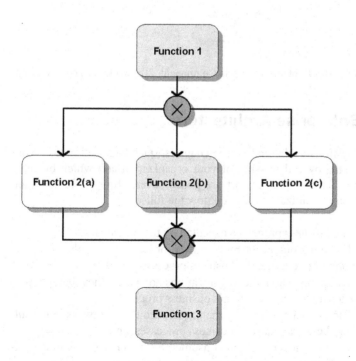

Figure 18.5 Analyst Consults the Services Repository

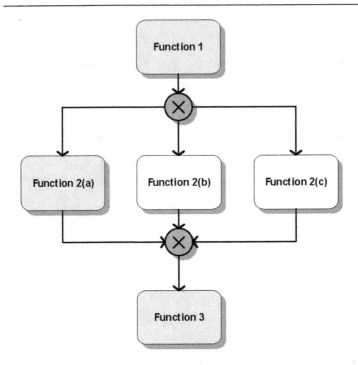

Figure 18.6 Analyst Replaces the As-Is Component, 2(b), with the To-Be Component, 2(a)

18.3 Enterprise Architecture

In the questions at the end of the chapters, questions asking how your job fits into the overall mission of your organization and which business process or processes you support are posed several times. Senior management of any organization should know the following:

- The business processes executed by the organization,
- The functions performed and the order in which they are performed to execute the business processes,
- The people and the organizations to which they belong who execute the organization's business processes,
- The IT systems used by the organization's employees in executing the organization's business processes, and
- The data generated and consumed by the IT systems in executing the organization's business processes

When the entire extended enterprise is to be captured, the data for the extended enterprise members should also be captured to the greatest extent possible.

How, one could ask, does an organization capture its business processes and the related information just described? A recommended way is through constructing an Enterprise Architecture.

A balanced scorecard may be considered an enterprise architecture as measured, in that an enterprise architecture defines the processes and subordinate functions to be performed and the balanced scorecard describes how they are measured. In fact, properly synchronized architectures and scorecards should contain the same basic information.

It is impossible, of course, to capture an organization of any size's business processes on a single product (known as "models.") Because of this, several different types of models have been developed:

- Functional- These models show only the functions that are executed. They may be in the order they are performed or may be listed as a group attached to a person, organization, IT system or business process.
- Organizational- These models may be as simple as an organization chart.
- IT System- These models could be as simple as a list of all systems owned by an organization. They could also include the functions fulfilled by the systems or it could even show the systems, and their functionalities in the "as-is" environment as well as the "to-be" environment.
- Data- Data models show the data generated by organizations, people and systems. In some instances they show the logical and/or physical schemas of the data.
- End-to-End Scenario (E2E)- These models show functions in the order they are performed with all possible variants for that scenario (defining scenarios so they are manageable in scope is a key skill to master) shown. Functions using an IT system are shown as being connected to it, and an IT system's owner is also shown.

There are several enterprise architecture tools in use to compose enterprise architectures, the best of which is ARIS, from IDS Scheer.

18.4 Enterprise Architecture Rationale

But why, one might ask, would one need to take the time to architect an entire extended enterprise? Why would we need to go through the trouble when we are getting along just fine as we are?

The answer is threefold: the Control Environment required by regulators and desired by investors, the anticipated transition to an SOA and portfolio management.

18.4.1 The Control Environment

As discussed in Chapter 8, the Sarbanes-Oxley (SOX) compliance regime has become a major issue with many corporations, as its Section 404 requires the CEO and CFO to certify personally that the company is truthfully reporting its financial data and that the company has a process in place to know the numbers are truthful. Compliance was much more expensive than originally anticipated, and exceptionally painful. Wagner and Dittmar (2006) note that some companies' processes differed by division, such as for when billing dates, dunning notices and interest charges were applied. This might have been irrelevant if the differences were between different companies, but they could have had a real impact on the consistency of the company's financial statements. By going through the trouble of documenting the organization's business processes, these discrepancies were able to be addressed. A second company noted that they were able to reduce the number of procedures for all financial journal entries from hundreds of ad hoc methods to three by mandating that all journal entries be made in the company's SAP system.

Another chance for improvement comes in minimizing human error. It is very easy for a human being to make a mistake when entering data into an unstructured (free-form) field. If on the other hand, only a string of characters configured a specific way is allowed, the user will not be able to complete their transaction until the IT system is satisfied.

Wagner and Dittmar (ibid) note that there are two types of controls: preventive and detective. Preventive controls are, as the name suggests, designed to stop unauthorized information from occurring. Physical security is one key element of the preventive control regime, as is the use of strong log-in authentication for systems and tight control of permissions throughout the enterprise. Even initial employee communication, executive communication and training are forms of preventive controls. Detective controls allow abuses to be discovered after the fact, such as through auditing who is accessing the system and viewing which data.

What is key to the enterprise architecture, however, is the SOX requirement to test controls. If the organization has taken the time to document its business processes thoroughly, the resulting E2Es would enable the organization to compose a test script for the organization. Because, as Wagner and Dittmar mention, there is no need to test more than a representative sample of business processes, a wide array of pre-modeled E2Es removes much of the stress from the requirement.

18.4.2 The SOA Transition

While not all organizations will be making the transition to an SOA in the near-term, architecting ones extended enterprise and keeping it current will facilitate the transition when it comes time to do so. The major concept to keep in mind here is that each and every piece of data generated and every bit of functionality in an SOA comes from a single source. This "single source of truth" means that a 100% accurate registry of data and services must be maintained at all times in order for the SOA to function properly.

Without a properly architected enterprise, it would be impossible to identify the people executing the organization's business processes and their functionality and data requirements.

18.4.3 Portfolio Management

Organizations are constantly faced with a decision as to when they will replace IT systems. How much are they "locked in"? In other words, is the sheer amount of money already sunk into fielding the current system so large that it would make no sense to replace it, or would the benefits of installing the new system be so great that it is justified no matter what the sunk cost of the legacy system?

In determining the IT systems to be kept and/or replaced, an organization must have an accurate picture of which systems they have, how much they cost to develop, upgrade and operate, and which business processes they support (this is known as a "portfolio of systems"). In documenting the status quo, the "as-is" architecture, senior management should be careful to avoid the "system replacement" trap, which is when candidate replacement systems are evaluated solely on their ability to replace the functionality offered by the legacy system. In the case of ERPs such as SAP and Oracle the functionality available will often far outpace that offered by the in-place system and will provide integration for all processes it implements. One type analysis, "gap-fit," is conducted when the current system functionality is seen as going away, which creates the gap. The best type of analysis, though, is "gap-plus" (Gulledge, 2004), which shows not only how well the candidate system takes over the legacy system but how it also accomplishes other processes currently supported by legacy systems.

> **Important:** Leaving a system turned on or shutting it off is not an "either/or" proposition! In many cases some functionality may be turned off and others left on. Be certain what may and may not be shut off before making a final portfolio decision.

18.5 Conclusion

The role of network security policies and procedures in a modern organization is a critical one. Unless excellent technical, physical and policy infrastructures are in place to (preferably) prevent or detect security violations an organization and its employees could face real jeopardy. In the new world of the extended enterprise, there is a real risk that the information captured could be used in to steal an identity or could be used to allow the thieves or their financial backers to build a product that the victim has put years of work into developing and beating them to market. After Enron and the other scandals of the Internet era, new regulations such as Sarbanes-Oxley are forcing companies to gain a much tighter control over their business processes and the information that is created and disseminated as they are executed. The best method to enable all policy areas discussed thus far and in the suggested policies in the next chapter is to create a complete architecture of the enterprise in which the organization rests. The first step is to document the organization itself, including:

- The business processes performed,
- The functions comprising the business processes,
- The people performing the functions and their organizational affiliation,
- The IT systems the people use to perform the functions, and

- The data accessed and generated by the person using the IT system as they perform their job.

Chapter 19 Draft Policies

Chapter Objectives

- This chapter will provide samples for use in formulating an organization's security-related policies. This is not intended as a full inventory of policies nor should any policy be adopted verbatim, as it is not the author's intent that you do so nor is the author able to attest that the draft policies would have any legal weight as he is not a lawyer.

19.1 Draft Policies

Page (2000) describes the seven sections of a policy document:

1. **"Purpose.** Explains objectives for writing a policy or procedure. Two or three sentences are adequate for this introductory paragraph. Do not include acronyms or technical terms that have yet to be defined in this heading.

2. **"Revision History.** Provides history of document changes whether they are minor typographical errors, major improvements, or re-engineering projects.

3. **"Persons Affected.** Provides a list of those persons or groups that might be impacted by the policy or procedure (i.e., target audiences or users). When all employees are affected, simply write, "All Employees." External groups like customers or suppliers should also be listed.

4. **"Policy.** Provides general organizational attitude of the organization; it reflects the basic objectives, goals, or vision. This is a good place to show the tie to business strategic goals. (*The inclusion of this statement within a procedure makes the proce-*

dure easier to understand without having to refer to another source for policy information.) [Emphasis in original.]

5. "**Definitions.** Provides explanations of abbreviations, acronyms, forms, words infrequently used, words not consistently understood, and technical terms. This is an important heading and should contain an explanation of the title, keywords, forms, references, and any exhibits. *(References can be placed in an exhibit and defined in this section.)* [Emphasis in original.]

6. "**Responsibilities.** Provides a short summary of the responsibilities of the individuals involved with a procedure. The specific title is generally used (e.g., Benefits Manager, CEO, or Buyer, the generic term, 'Employee,' can be used when necessary.) This section should be written in the same sequence of events that occurs under the 'Procedures' section.

7. "**Procedures.** Defines and outlines the rules, regulations, methods timing, place and personnel responsible for accomplishing the policy as stated in Section 4. This section should follow the process flow as described in the flow chart. The process is described from start to finish, including all the inputs, outputs, and value-added activities."

In this chapter, the purpose, persons affected, policy, responsibilities and procedures will be completed.

19.1.1 The Policy Policy

The first place to start, of course, is with a policy directing how policies are to be formed, reviewed and updated.

Purpose: Organizational policies must be identified and developed as required. Once established, policies must be reviewed and updated regularly.

Persons Affected: All employees.

Policy: The organization shall identify all areas in which policies are required and will assign the appropriate employees the task of composing and submitting them for review. A committee of senior executives will review all draft policies and will either approve their adoption or forward them to the overall responsible party (Company owner, for example) for final approval.

Responsibilities: All employees are expected to understand the policies impacting their positions and shall recommend new policies or changes to existing policies based on two factors: best facilitating the organization's support of its customers/constituency, and protecting the organization and its employees against the impact of intentional and unintentional improper behavior on the part of one or more of its employees.

Customer-facing employees are expected to draft policies that will help guide current and future employees in providing the best service possible while ensuring the organization's security is protected to the greatest extent possible.

Managers shall evaluate customer-facing policies in the total context of how they impact their area of responsibility as a whole and recommend changes to existing and draft policies as well as new policies based on their assessment of their position and in providing the best balance of customer service and organizational security. Managers are authorized to give final approval to policies in their area of responsibility so long as they do not conflict with policies governing the overall business of the organization.

Senior executives are expected to evaluate or supervise the evaluation of policies that are currently in force within the organization every six months for currency. After two six-month reviews, policies shall be assigned individual review dates. Senior executives are also expected to generate policies governing their areas of responsibility and evaluate their impacts on the organization's executing its business processes while ensuring security is maintained.

Procedures: When employees join the organization and when they assume a position in a division for the first time they are expected to be provided with, read and sign a statement confirming a statement that they understand the policies currently in force that affect them.

The organization shall ensure that every employee has immediate access to the policies governing their position in either hard (paper) or soft (electronic media, computer) format.

Employees shall compose draft new or revised policies as required or as they feel necessary and submit them to their manager for review and possible adoption or forwarding to the next level of review.

Managers shall review all policies in their area of responsibility every six months for currency and relevance. Special emphasis shall be placed on ensuring that all contact information for persons to be reached outside of normal operating hours is current.

Senior executives shall draft and approve or submit for approval policies affecting the overall operating philosophy of the organization. When formulating draft policies, emphasis shall be placed on ensuring the organization's defined business processes are enacted in such a way that security is maintained. A portion of each senior executive committee meeting will be reserved for policy review.

19.1.2 Business Process Documentation Policy

Purpose: An organization's business processes must be understood fully by all entitled to the information. To ensure all understand or are able to access business process information, all organizational business processes shall be documented in an Enterprise Architecture.

Persons Affected: All employees.

Policy: All of the organization's business processes shall be documented in the form of an Enterprise Architecture (EA). The EA shall contain the following information:

- All business processes performed by the organization,
- All individual functions performed, in the order they are performed, in implementing the business processes,
- The positions (not an individual's name) responsible for performing each individual function,
- The part (department) organization to which that position belongs,
- The reporting relationship of that part of the organization with the other departments,
- The IT system or systems used to perform a function,
- The data created or accessed by the IT system or systems in performing the function, and

- Outside parties (partners, vendors, customers, for example) with which information is exchanged when executing the organization's business processes.

For all positions, the least amount of access privilege required to perform their duties shall be determined and that level of access shall be granted to the user.

Responsibilities: Senior executives shall define the organization's business processes at a high level, leveraging to the greatest extent possible existing reference architectures.

Managers shall work with senior executives to validate the high-level business processes and shall then supervise and participate in defining the business processes down to each individual action taken by an employee in executing a business process. Several "levels" of models could be required to ensure each individual model is understandable.

Employees shall work with managers to validate the granular business processes and will recommend when a change in business processes would be justified.

To facilitate reporting and architecture analysis, an EA tool, such as ARIS, shall be used in composing the architecture.

At each level, security concerns shall be noted and their processes shall be incorporated in the EA.

Procedures: Senior executives shall participate in workshops to develop the EA models depicting the organization's overarching business processes.

Managers shall participate in workshops to validate the high-level business process models and will participate in other workshops to compose more granular models down to the individual process step level.

Employees shall participate in workshops to compose EA products depicting the functions they perform, the systems they use and the positions and outside parties with which they exchange information in performing their jobs.

Who is authorized to add, edit and delete data into systems must be defined. The only way to properly establish these roles is through a thorough understanding of the organization's business processes to know who person or which job is the "single source of truth" for each piece of data going into the system and the level of permissions they need to be able to do their job.

19.1.3 Awareness Training

In addition to the specific, compliance-based training, general security training is required of all employees, including those who may not have access to sensitive information as part of their jobs. As Peltier (2005) notes, there are five key elements to an information security awareness program. They are:

1. "A process to take the message to the user community to reinforce the concept that information security is an important part of the business process.
2. "Identification of the individuals who are responsible for the implementation of the security program.
3. "The ability to determine the sensitivity of information and the criticality of applications, systems and business processes.
4. "The business reasons why basic security concepts such as separation of duties, need-to-know, and least privilege must be implemented.
5. "That senior management supports the goals and objectives of the information security program."

Purpose: To ensure that all employees are aware of basic security concepts and responsibilities, information security awareness training shall be developed and given. All employees are required to complete this training satisfactorily before beginning their jobs.

Persons Affected: All employees.

Policy: The training material shall be delivered in such a way as to ensure that all employees are aware of their role in protecting organizational security.

Overviews of the various compliance regimes shall be provided.

Sensitive information shall not be provided based on a verbal request alone. An email request is sufficient, and if an employee receives a verbal request they should send an email stating the information to be provided and should not actually provide the information unless and until they receive an email response from the requestor confirming the requirement.

Sensitive information shall not be provided to anyone, including senior executives, not entitled to it. Should there be any question on the part of the employee who received the request, they should inquire of their supervisor as to the proper course of action and not act until they have received direction.

At no point is it ever permissible for an employee to access information or IT systems for which they are not authorized regardless of who is making the request.

Responsibilities: Senior executives are responsible for establishing the high-level priorities of the training program.

Managers are responsible for working with the trainers to develop the training material.

The trainers, whether internal or external to the organization, are responsible for developing and delivering the training material.

Employees are responsible for completing the training diligently and for putting the training into practice in their jobs.

"Refresher" training to re-enforce the concepts presented shall be provided on a periodic basis.

Jobs requiring specific security procedures shall have a separate training regimen developed and delivered.

Procedures: Senior executives shall participate in workshops to establish the information security awareness training priorities.

Management shall work with the trainers and compliance authority to develop training material and shall validate the material with the senior executives.

Employees shall attend the training and shall sign a statement that they have received and understand the material presented to them.

"Refresher" training shall be provided on yearly basis or more often as required.

The training material shall be reviewed and updated on a yearly basis or more often as required.

19.1.4 Regulatory Compliance

Purpose: Failure to comply with regulatory regimes can jeopardize the organization's ability to fulfill its mission and could expose the organization and individual employees to possible legal risk. The organization and its employees will be aware of and will adhere to the requirements of all regulations governing organizational conduct.

Persons Affected: All employees with access to sensitive information.

Policy: All employees shall be aware of their responsibilities as it relates to regulations governing how organizations execute their business processes.

All employees will be trained on the proper execution of their job and will sign a statement acknowledging that they have received and understand the training. The training shall include:

- An overview of the various regulations governing their position,
- The information security requirements put in place to protect the employee from improperly disclosing information, and
- The business process steps to be performed so as to ensure all activity is auditable from a regulatory compliance perspective.

Senior executives shall be aware of their responsibilities in certifying that regulatory compliance has been achieved and the possible legal exposure the organization and they could face if the regulation has been violated.

Responsibilities: Managers shall ensure the training material is up-to-date and shall ensure that all employees receive "refresher" training yearly or more often as required.

Managers, senior executives and auditors shall ascertain where various compliance requirements overlap in order to avoid duplicative efforts as much as possible.

Employees will understand how regulatory requirements impact their job functions and shall always act in a way that complies with these requirements.

Procedures: Before an employee is allowed to begin a job requiring access to sensitive information they will be trained on how to handle the data properly.

The processes involved in all compliance efforts will be architected and overlaps and chances for consolidating efforts will be analyzed.

In preparation for periodic audits, such as the testing of the organization's control environment, test scenarios shall be composed and executed. The results shall be evaluated and lessons learned shall be applied for both compliance and business process improvement purposes.

Senior executives charged with attesting to the veracity of the information provided to the compliance authority shall establish a process through which they are able to provide their attestation.

For the remainder of the topics, the procedures have been omitted...

19.1.5 Physical Security

Purpose: To ensure that the organization's facilities are protected as well as possible from penetration by unauthorized persons, controls on access to each facility must be put in place. Additionally, items capable of recording, storing and removing sensitive information from an organization facility will not be allowed into the facility at the sole discretion of the organization.

Persons Affected: All employees.

Policy: Physical access to the organization's facilities is to be controlled at all times.

Access to the facility shall not be permitted through an unlocked or unmonitored entrance.

All employees shall wear a badge with a current picture, first and last name, and any special levels of access.

All visitors are required to sign in, which will also serve as an acknowledgment that the organization has the right to inspect any IT device suspected of storing sensitive organizational data.

All visitors are required to declare any items determined by the organization to be "controlled" to the organization and to allow them to be stored while the visitor is in the facility.

All visitors will be issued a distinctive badge, which will indicate clearly that they are a visitor and whether or not an escort is required.

Areas in which classified or proprietary work is performed will be secured in accordance with government of company policy.

Security will conduct random inspections, in which proper badge display, visitor escort policy and whether classified or proprietary information is improperly secured will be checked.

All IT equipment shall be stored in a part of the facility accessible with unique keys or access cards.

All backup materials shall be transported securely and the security practices of outside companies shall be audited.

IT equipment shall be inventoried monthly or more often as required.

Responsibilities: The security office shall develop draft security procedures and shall validate them with senior management.

Human resources shall ensure that all security training has been received and that all proper forms and acknowledgements have been completed.

Managers shall monitor their employees to ensure physical security procedures are being followed.

All employees shall report suspicious activity to their supervisor or the security office immediately.

19.1.6 Disaster Recovery

Purpose: While the risk of an event that would significantly disrupt operations is slight on a daily basis, it is expected that over time at least one incident will cause an interruption in daily business. As such, it is critical to know beforehand how the organization will conduct its business.

Persons Affected: All employees.

Policy: As many potential causes of significant business disruption ("disasters") shall be identified and scenarios to recover and to continue doing business with as little disruption as possible will be developed. The business processes developed as a part of the enterprise architecture shall be leveraged to help determine the best course of action.

The organization shall have adequate insurance coverage to ensure all damages are covered.

Each employee shall have a current list of other employees' contact information in order to facilitate the prompt notification of an incident. This list shall be validated every six months as well as when new employees join the organization or when employees leave.

A Business Continuity Team will be formed and will be trained to respond to incidents from the organization's perspective.

Alternate communication/IT connectivity services shall be ready to be used in case the primary work site is unavailable.

The priority and order of IT system restoration shall be determined by studying the role each system plays in the organization's business processes.

Data shall be backed up and secured at a location outside the facility.

Controls over regulated, classified and proprietary data shall be anticipated and established for business continuity.

Responsibilities: Senior executives shall establish the business continuity process and shall appoint managers to be in charge of the aspects of the plan within their area of responsibility.

Managers shall know through developing and having access to potential disaster scenarios how to respond to most crises.

All employees shall inform their points of contact of the disaster and shall perform their functions as detailed in the business continuity plan.

19.1.7 Initial Employee Communication

Purpose: When an employee joins an organization, it is best to establish the proper level of expectation and responsibilities the employee will have relative to ensuring security and protecting sensitive information. Through the use of training material and legal documents, an organization makes clear what the employee may expect of the organization and what the organization will expect of the employee in return.

Persons Affected: All employees

Policy: Human Resources shall work with senior management to create an employee agreement to be signed by all new hires as a condition of employment. The agreement shall be tailored to apply to the jurisdiction of the organization's choosing. The employee shall agree to not disclose any confidential information and to adhere to all information security policies and procedures.

If not included in the employee agreement, the employee shall sign a Non-Disclosure Agreement (NDA) stating that they will keep safe all protected information related to their job.

Should the employee be working in a position of trust, an additional document affirming that the employee shall adhere to position-specific policies shall be signed.

The employee shall be made aware that should they be found to have violated any laws that they will be individually responsible for responding to any legal inquiries and responding to any criminal charges.

The employee shall be informed of the organization's right to monitor all activity on its network and to inspect any device used to access the network regardless of whether the device was issued to the employee by the organization or is the employee's personally owned machine.

The employee shall be informed of the organization's policy on accessing personal email, surfing the Internet and making personal phone calls during business hours.

Responsibilities: Human Resources shall draft policy documents and coordinate with the organization's legal team and senior management to ensure the employee agreement is legally enforceable.

Senior managers shall ensure training is developed and provided to enable employees to fulfill the promises made in their employee agreement.

Employees shall understand the requirements they have levied on them by the employee agreement, the NDA, and any other policy document that is required for employment.

19.1.8 Email and Instant Messaging

Purpose: Email and Instant Messaging (IM) are major methods of communication in modern business and personal life. Because of its popularity, ease of use and relative lack of security, email and IM have been attacked by, among others, hackers and social engineers attempting to gain access to systems and user-supplied information. This policy establishes acceptable use and monitoring practices for the organization.

Persons Affected: All employees.

Policy: All emails and IMs sent from organization machines or over organization networks are the property of the organization.

Personal email and IM is to be limited and is not, under any circumstances, to interfere with the employee's fulfilling their duties.

No email or IM is to be used to transmit, discuss or view material that is pornographic, racist or offensive in any way.

All messages sent from an organization-owned machine or sent over the organization's network shall be archived in a repository for efficient retrieval if required.

Retrieval capability shall be tested periodically.

A user has no right to privacy as to emails and IMs sent from an organization-owned machine or over an organization network.

Password standards for IM shall be the same as for email.

No proprietary, classified or otherwise controlled information is to be disseminated over the network unless the requirements of the position's specific release policy validates the method of the request.

Responsibilities: Each employee is responsible for knowing what information is prohibited from being disseminated over email or IM.

Senior executives and managers are responsible for determining what information may not be disseminated over email or IM.

Each employee is responsible for ensuring their personal email or IM does not interfere with their duties.

The IT department is responsible for ensuring all email and IM traffic is monitored and archived when required.

19.1.9 Network Access

Purpose: Access to the organization's networks must be controlled carefully. Because of the danger of an unauthorized person accessing the organization's networks, this policy must be enforced rigidly.

Persons Affected: IT, all employees

Policy: Only authorized users may be issued user accounts. All of the organization's employees will be issued accounts and shall use their organization account to perform all business functions.

All users will be assigned a user role based on their position and will enjoy only those privileges granted to that role unless written authorization from a senior manager is received.

Under no circumstances shall an employee divulge any login information to an organization network to anyone not authorized to know it.

When an employee leaves the organization, their account shall be deactivated within six hours of the end of their last day.

Passwords must be a minimum of eight characters long and must contain at least (number) of special characters.

All default passwords must be changed immediately upon initial use.

Accounts with anonymous user names are not allowed to access the organization's networks.

Responsibilities: The IT department shall establish user roles in consultation with senior executives and management.

The IT department shall establish the requirements for an acceptable user password.

The IT department is responsible for removing or disabling default accounts on items.

Each user is responsible for protecting their login information from disclosure.

Bibliography

Acheson, James; "Welcome to Nobel Country: A Review of Institutional Economics"; in *Anthropology and Institutional Economics*; Monographs in Economic Anthropology, No. 12; James Acheson, ed.; University Press of America; Lanham, MD; 1994

The American Heritage Dictionary of the English Language: Fourth Edition; 2000; Houghton Mifflin Company; www.dictionary.com.

Anthes, Gary; "The Future of Email"; June 12, 2006; downloaded from www.computerworld.com, June 29, 2006

Arrow, K.J.; *The Limits of Organization*; Norton, New York, NY; 1974

Associated Press; "E-Discovery is Big Business"; January 29, 2006; downloaded from www.wired.com January 30, 2006

Baker, Mark C., Charles A. Witschorik, Jonathan C. Tuch, Waverly Hagey-Espie, Veena B. Mendiratta; "Architectures and Disaster Recovery Strategies for Survivable Telecommunication Services"; *Bell Labs Technical Journal*; Vol. 9, No. 2; 2004

Barman, Scott; *Writing Information Security Policies*; New Riders; Indianapolis, IN; 2002

Batts, Nathan; "404 Means Huge Costs for Questionable Gains"; *American Banker*; April 29, 2005; Vol. 170, No. 82; p. 10

Bednarz, Ann; "Offsite Security Complicates Compliance"; *Network World*; March 21, 2005; Vol. 22, No. 11; pp. 27-28

Benanto, Ron; "Reducing Risk Through Data Auditing"; *Financial Executive*; April, 2005; Vol. 21, No. 3; pp. 58-60

Berti, John; "Social Engineering: The Forgotten Risk"; *Canadian HR Reporter*; July 14, 2003; Vol. 16, Issue 3; pg. 21

Blum, Daniel; "Risk Management, Controls Key to SOX" (also: "Risk mgmt., controls key to SOX); *Network World*; May 2, 2005; Vol. 22, No. 17; p. 51

Britt, Phillip; "Ethical Hackers: Testing the Security Waters"; *Information Today*; September, 2005; Vol. 22, No. 8; p. 1

Chuvakin, Anton; "Honeypot Essentials"; *Telecommunications, Network Security, and Internet Security*; January/February, 2003

Coase, Ronald; "The Nature of the Firm"; *Economica*; November, 1937; No. 4; p. 386-405

Coe, Barbara A.; "How Structural Conflicts Stymie Reinvention"; *Public Administration Review*; Vol. 57, No. 2; 1997; pp. 168-173

Coe, Kathleen; "Closing the Security Gap"; *HR Magazine*; Vol. 48, No. 8; August, 2003; p. 95

Coe, Martin J.; "Sarbanes-Oxley: Executive Summary"; *Journal of Accountancy*; March, 2005; Vol. 199, No. 3; p. 70

"Compliance Driving IT Budgets"; anonymous; downloaded from www.sap.info April 11, 2006

ComputerWeekly.com; "Strategy Clinic: How Can You Test Disaster Recovery Plans?"; June 9, 2004; downloaded from ComputerWeekly.com June 3, 2006

Condon, Ron; "What's the Next Security Threat?"; April 17, 2006; downloaded from www.news.com, April 17, 2006

Crowe, Michael R. and Kelly Canavan; "Recent Legal Developments: Analysis of Enforcement Activities under Sarbanes-Oxley"; *Journal of Healthcare Compliance*; May/June, 2005; Vol. 7, No. 3; pp. 5-12

Darrow, Barbara; "E-Mail Regs Still Driving Business" *CRN*; May 16, 2005; Issue 1147; p. 29

Dhamija, Rachna, J.D. Tygar and Marti Hearst; "Why Phishing Works"; *Presented to CHI Conference, April 20-27, 2006; Montreal, Canada*

Donaldson, L.; "The Ethereal Hand: Organizational Economics and Management Theory"; *Academy of Management Review*; Rev. 15, No. 3; 1990; pp. 369-381

Dorf, John and Marty Johnson; "Restoration Component of Business Continuity Planning"; in Tipton, Harold F. and Micki Krause (editors); *Information Security Management Handbook*; 4th Edition; Auerbach; Boca Raton, FL; 2000

Dubberly, David; "Non-Disclosure Agreements Protect Competitive Edge"; *South Carolina Business Journal*; August, 1998; Vol. 17, No. 7 August, 1998

Eisenhardt, K.M.; "Agency and Institutional Theory Explanations: The Case of Retail Sales Compensation"; *Academy of Management Journal*; 1988; Vol. 31, No. 2; pp. 488-511

Engle, Paul; "Managing Risk"; *Industrial Engineer*; May, 2005; Vol. 37, No. 5; p. 22

Ensuring   E-mail   Security;   undated;   downloaded   from www.networkworld.com; June 15, 2006

Erlanger, Leon; "The Weakest Link"; *PC Magazine*; March 16, 2004; downloaded from www.pcmag.com/solutions

Evers, Joris; "ChoicePoint Overhaul Falls Behind"; June 24, 2005; downloaded from www.news.com July 1, 2005

Evers, Joris; "Details Emerge on Credit Card Breach"; June 20, 2005; downloaded from www.news.com July 1, 2005

Frauenheim, Ed; "Relief from Sarbanes-Oxley on the Way?"; June 9, 2005; downloaded from www.news.com June 25, 2006

Fritz, Robert; *Corporate Tides*; Berrett-Koehler; San Francisco, CA; 1996

Frye, Douglas W.; *Electronic Procurement in the Private and Public Sectors*; Doctoral Dissertation, George Mason University, School of Public Policy; April, 2004

Gage, Deborah and Kim S. Nash; "Security Alert: When Bots Attack"; April 6, 2006; downloaded from www.baselinemag.com April 9, 2006

Gilman, Joel B.; "When an Employee Leaves, Make Sure His Knowledge Stays"; *Systems Integration*; December, 1990; Vol. 23, No. 2

Greenwald, Judy; "Electronic Security Threats Come from Outside and Within"; *Business Insurance*; May 23, 2005; Vol. 39, No. 21; pp. 11-12

Grimes, Roger A.; "Encryption for All: Protecting Your Hard Drives will Help Keep Your Company from Getting Snakebit by Security Breaches"; March 31, 2006; downloaded from www.infoworld.com April 3, 2006

Gulledge, Thomas; personal communication, 2004

Hagenbaugh, Barbara and Matt Krantz; "New Accounting Rules Raise Price of Audits: Cost of Compliance Takes Toll on Companies"; *USA Today*; April 13, 2005; p. B1

Hines, Matt; "New Phishing Attack Uses Real ID Hooks"; May 15, 2005; downloaded from www.news.com June 20, 2005

Holstein, William J.; "In Defense of Sarbox"; *Chief Executive*; May, 2005; Issue 208; pp. 36-38

Hope, Michele; "Who's Minding the Store?"; in *Ensuring E-mail Security*; undated; downloaded from www.networkworld.com; June 15, 2006

Houston, Douglas A.; "Trust in a Networked Economy: Doing Business on Web Time"; *Business* Horizons; March-April, 2001; Vol. 44, No. 2; pp. 38-44

House Report 105-851: Report of the Select Committee on U.S. National Security and Military/Commercial Concerns With The People's Republic of China; (also known as *The Cox Report*); 1999; http://www.gpo.gov/congress/house/hr105851-html

IMLogic Threat Center; *2005 Real-Time Communication Security: The Year in Review*; downloaded from www.imlogic.com June 30, 2006

IMLogic Threat Center; *Managing Instant Messaging for Business Advantage: Phase Two: Protecting Against IM Threats*; downloaded from www.imlogic.com June 30, 2006

IMLogic Threat Center; *Top 5 Instant Messaging Security Risks for 2006*; downloaded from www.imlogic.com June 30, 2006

Imperato, Gabriel L.; "Corporate Crime, Responsibility, and Compliance and Governance"; *Journal of Health Care Compliance*; May/June, 2005; Vol. 7, No. 3; pp. 11-18

Isaza, John J.; "Know When to Hold 'Em, When to Destroy 'Em"; *Information Management Journal*; March/April, 2005; Vol. 39, No. 2; pp. 39-43

Iskat, Gregory and Jay Liebowitz; "What To Do When Employees Resist Change"; *SuperVision*; August, 2003; Vol. 64, No. 8; p. 12

Jackson, Carl B.; "Reengineering the Business Continuity Planning Process"; in Tipton, Harold F. and Micki Krause (editors); *Information Security Management Handbook*; 4th Edition; Auerbach; Boca Raton, FL; 2000

Jacoba, Ronald L. and Michael J. Jones; *Structured-On-The-Job Training*; Berrett-Koehler Publishers; San Francisco, CA; 1995

Joint Inquiry Into Intelligence Community Activities Before and After the Terrorist Attacks of September 11, 2001; *Report of the U.S. Senate Select Committee on Intelligence and the U.S. House Permanent Select Committee on Intelligence: Additional Views of Members of the Joint Inquiry*;   December,   2002; http://files.findlaw.com/news.findlaw.com/hdocs/docs/911rpt/911report72403.pdf

Jones, Chris; *Social Engineering: Understanding and Auditing*; GSEC, v1.4b, Option #1; November 4, 2003; SANS Institute

Keizer, Gregg; "Rootkits to Mask Most Malware by 2008"; April 21, 2006; downloaded from www.techweb.com April 22, 2006

Kim, Eyong B.; "Information Security Awareness Status of Full Time Employees"; *The Business Review, Cambridge*; Summer, 2005; Vol. 3, No. 2; p. 219

Kirschniak, Christian; "Complex Projects Under Control"; April 3, 2006; downloaded from www.sap.info April 3, 2006

Knight, Amy W.; *Spies without Cloaks: The KGB's Successors*; Princeton University Press; Princeton, NJ; 1997

Koestenbaum, Peter, Patrick J. Keys and Thomas R. Weirich; "Integrating Sarbanes-Oxley, Leadership, and Ethics"; *The CPA Journal*; April, 2005; Vol. 75, No. 4; pp. 13-15

Krebs, Brian; "Hacking Made Easy: Automated Tools Gather Victims' Keystrokes, Upload Passwords to Illicit Database"; March 16, 2006; downloaded from www.washingtonpost.com March 16, 2006

Kuczynski, Kay and Patty Gibbs-Wahlberg; "HIPAA the Health Care Hippo: Despite the Rhetoric, is Privacy Still an Issue?"; *Social Work*; Vol. 50, No. 3; July, 2005; pp. 283-287

Lamont, Judith; "Managing Content for Compliance"; *KM World*; March, 2005; Vol. 14, No. 3; pp. 12-14

Leibenstein, Harvey; *Beyond Economic Man: A New Foundation for Microeconomics*; Harvard University Press; Cambridge, MA; 1976

Leibenstein, Harvey; *General X-Inefficiency Theory and Economic Development*; Oxford University Press; London, UK; 1978

Leibenstein, Harvey; *Inside the Firm: The Inefficiencies of Hierarchy*; Harvard University Press; Cambridge, MA; 1987

Leon, Mark; "Hard Won Lessons from the Compliance Front"; *Infoworld*; April 4. 2005; Vol. 27, No. 14; pp. 42-46

Lewin, Kurt; "Group Decision and Social Change"; in *Readings in Social Philosophy*; rev. ed.; G.E. Swanson, T.N. Newcomb, and E.L. Hartley; Holt, New York, NY; 1952

Libbey, Miles; "Email Authentication Proposal—DKIM—Fights Phishing and Email Forgery"; in *Ensuring E-mail Security*; undated; downloaded from www.networkworld.com; June 15, 2006

Lively, Charles E., Jr.; *Psychological Based Social Engineering*; GSEC Option 1, Version 1.4b; SANS Institute; December, 2003

Mannan, Mohammad; "Secure Public Instant Messaging"; Masters Thesis; downloaded
Mannan, Mohammad and Paul C. van Oorschot; "On Instant Messaging Worms, Analysis and Countermeasures"; presented at *WORM '05*; November 11, 2005; Fairfax, VA; USA

Marson, Ingrid; "Marriott Loses Data on 200,000 Customers"; January 3, 2006; accessed from www.news.com, January 7, 2006

McCoy, Carrie and Rebecca Thurmond Fowler; "'You Are the Key to Security': Establishing a Successful Security Awareness Program"; Presented at SIGUCCS '04; Baltimore, MD; October 10-13, 2004

McMaster, Robert and John W. Sawkins; "The Contract State, Trust Distortion and Efficiency"; *Review of Social Economy*; Summer 1996; Vol. 54, No. 2; p. 145

McLaughlin, Kevin; "Symantec Addresses IM Security, Compliance"; March 31, 2006; downloaded from www.crn.com April 3, 2006

McNamara, Paul; "Encryption & Plugging Data Leaks"; in *Ensuring E-mail Security*; undated; downloaded from www.networkworld.com; June 15, 2006

Millard, Elizabeth; "Phishers Using New Methods to Steal User Information"; May 5, 2005; downloaded from www.newsfactor.com June 20, 2005

Mitnick, Kevin D. and William L. Simon; *The Art of Deception: Controlling the Human Element of Security*; Wiley; Indianapolis, IN; 2002

Musthaler, Linda; "Microsoft Enables Administrators to Block all Email Attachments"; in *Ensuring E-mail Security*; undated; downloaded from www.networkworld.com; June 15, 2006

Naraine, Ryan; "Government Funded Startup Blasts Rootkits"; April 24, 2006; downloaded from www.eweek.com April 25, 2006

Newsfactor.com; "The Hidden Dangers of Instant Messaging"; July 5, 2006; downloaded from www.newsfactor.com, July 5, 2006

North, Douglass C.; "Institutions and Credible Commitment"; *Journal of Institutional and Theoretical Economics*; (Symposium on the New Institutional Economics); 1993; No. 149 (1); pp. 11-23

North, Douglass C.; *Institutions, Institutional Change and Economic Performance*; Cambridge University Press; Cambridge, UK; 1990

Orgill, Gregory, Gordon W. Romney, Michael G. Bailey and Paul M. Orgill; "The Urgency for Effective User Privacy-education to Counter Social Engineering Attacks on Secure Computer Systems"; Presented to the Association for Computing Machinery's SIGITE '04 conference; October 28-30, 2004; ISBN 1-58113-936-5/04/10

Osterman, Michael; "Making the Case with Higher-Ups for Email Encryption Isn't Always Easy"; in *Ensuring E-mail Security*; undated; downloaded from www.networkworld.com; June 15, 2006

Page, Stephen B.; *Achieving 100% Compliance of Policies and Procedures*; Process Improvement Publishing; Westerville, OH; 2000

Peltier, Thomas R.; "Implementing an Information Security Awareness Program"; *Information Systems Security*; May/June, 2005; Vol. 14, No. 2; p. 37

Peltier, Thomas R.; "Social Engineering: Concepts and Solutions"; *EDPACS*; February, 2006; Vol. 33, No. 8; p. 1

Perelman, Michael; "Competition: The Hidden Costs of the Invisible Hand"; *Challenge*; March, 2001; Vol. 44, No. 2; p. 85

Rabe, Jens; "The Layers of Email Management"; *KM World*; March, 2005; Vol. 14, No. 3; pp. S6-7

Ranger, Steve; "Report: Sarbanes-Oxley Could Threaten Security"; July 11, 2005; downloaded from ww.news.com July 11, 2005

Rohan, Rebecca; "Social Engineering"; *Black Enterprise*; September, 2002; Vol. 33, No. 2; p. 53

Roberts, Paul F.; "Spear Phishing Attack Targets Credit Unions"; December 16, 2005; downloaded from www.eweek.com January 9, 2006

Rutberg, Sidney; "Disaster Recovery"; *Secured Lender*; March/April, 2005; Vol. 61, No. 2; p. 30

Sako, Mari; *Prices, Quality and Trust: Interfirm Relations in Britain and Japan*; Cambridge University Press; Cambridge, UK; 1992

Schein, Edgar H.; "Models and Tools for Stability and Change in Human Systems"; *Reflections*; Vol. 4, No. 2; 2002

Schneider, Carl E.; "HIPAA-cracy"; *Hastings Center Report*; January/February, 2006; Vol. 36, No. 1; pp. 10-11

Sheffi, Yossi; *The Resilient Enterprise: Overcoming Vulnerability for Competitive Advantage*; MIT Press; Cambridge, MA; 2005

Shelton, J.P.; "Allocative Efficiency vs. X-Efficiency—Comment"; *American Economic Review*; No. 57; 1967; pp. 1252-1258

Solomon, Deborah and Diya Gullapalli; "Moving the Market: Auditors Get Sarbanes-Oxley Rebuke"; *Wall Street Journal (Eastern Edition)*; May 17, 2005; p. C3

Sterlicchi, John; "That Was the Year 2005"; March 20, 2006; downloaded from www.sap.info April 3, 2006

Stim, Richard and David Pressman; *Patent Pending in 24 Hours*; 3rd Edition; Nolo; Berkeley, CA; 2004

Sturgeon, Will; "The Secret of Phishers' Success"; April 3, 2006; downloaded from www.news.com April 3, 2006

Surowiecki, James; *The Wisdom of Crowds: Why the Many Are Smarter than the Few and How Collective Wisdom Shapes Business, Economies, Societies, and Nations*; Doubleday; New York, NY; 2004

Svensson, Carsten and Doug Frye; "Enterprise Services Architecture as a Business Process Enabler"; *IFIP*; Rockville, MD, USA; September 21, 2005

Tapscott, Don; *Growing Up Digital: The Rise of the Net Generation*; McGraw-Hill, New York, NY; 1997

Terreri, April; "Securing Your Company's Data"; *Business NH Magazine*; September 1, 2004; Vol. 21, No. 9; p. 24

Tipton, Harold F. and Micki Krause (editors); *Information Security Management Handbook*; 4th Edition; Auerbach; Boca Raton, FL; 2000

Trembly, Ara C.; "Phishing Threatens Agents, Carriers, Insureds"; *National Underwriter*; February 21, 2005; Vol. 109, No. 7; pp. 11-12

Tyson, Jeff; "How Encryption Works"; downloaded from computer.howstuffworks.com, April 18, 2006

Vijayan, Jaikumar; "Progress is Slow on HIPAA Security Rules"; *Computerworld*; September 12, 2005; Vol. 39, No. 37; p. 69

Wagner, Stephen and Lee Dittmar; "The Unexpected Benefits of Sarbanes-Oxley"; *Harvard Business Review*; April, 2006; Vol. 84, No. 4; pp. 133-140

Ward, Hazel; "Bosses Voice E-Procurement Fears"; *Computer Weekly*; July 20, 2000; p. 16; downloaded from www.computerweekly.com July 22, 2002

Wetty, Bill and Irma Becerra-Fernandez; "Managing Trust and Commitment in Collaborative Supply Chain Relationships"; *Communications of the ACM*; June, 2001; Vol. 44, No. 6; p. 67

Wetzel, Rebecca; "Tackling Phishing"; *Business Communications Review*; Vol. 35, No. 2; pp. 46-49

"Will Enron's Legacy Benefit Business?"; downloaded from knowledge.emory.edu May 17, 2006

Wired.com; "CitiFinancial Data Goes Poof"; June 6, 2005; downloaded from www.wired.com, June 6, 2005

Worthy, Susan; "The Case for Active Archiving"; *KM World*; March, 2005; Vol. 14, No. 3; p. S14

Wright, Peter and Ananda Mukherji; "Inside the Firm: Socioeconomic Versus Agency Perspectives on Firm Competitiveness"; *The Journal of Socio-Economics*; May, 1999; Vol. 28, No. 3; p. 295

Wrong, D. "The Oversocialized Concept of Man in Modern Sociology"; *American Economic Review*; Rev. 26, No. 2; 1961; pp. 183-193

www.bytepile.com/definitions-p.php, downloaded August 3, 2006

Yerkes, R. M. and J.D. Dodson; "The Relation of Strength of Stimulus to Rapidity of Habit Formation"; *Journal of Comparative Neurology and Psychology*; (18); 1908; pp. 459-482

Index